This journal
belongs to a
curious reader:

MENTAL FLOSS

THE CURIOUS READER A JOURNAL FOR BOOK LOVERS

by Erin McCarthy and the Team at Mental Floss

weldon**owen**

CEO Raoul Goff
PUBLISHER Roger Shaw
ASSOCIATE PUBLISHER Mariah Bear
EDITORIAL DIRECTOR Katie Killebrew
ART DIRECTOR Allister Fein
VP MANUFACTURING Alix Nicholaeff
PRODUCTION MANAGER Andy Harper

weldon**owen**

PO Box 3088
San Rafael, CA 94912
www.weldonowen.com

© 2021 Sportority Inc.
ISBN 978-1-68188-772-2
Produced by Indelible Editions

INDELIBLE
EDITIONS

Printed in China
10 9 8 7 6 5 4 3 2 1
2021 2022 2023 2024

CONTENTS

INTRODUCTION

If you're anything like the Mental Floss team, you probably find organizing your bookshelves an invigorating activity. Physically reordering all those volumes—whether by author, title, genre, or some other system—kickstarts a similar mental decluttering: an automatic inventory of what you've read, what struck you most about each book, what you'd like to read next, and so on. Not only can that feel cathartic, it can also remind you why you love books.

The Curious Reader Journal for Book Lovers can be a continuation of that process. Within its pages you'll find prompts that help you pay closer attention to what you read and how you choose your books. There are also pages where you can list your favorite works, track your reading progress, and jot down your own ideas and reflections. And since it's from Mental Floss, you'll also find memorable quotes, fascinating facts about novels and novelists, and what it's called when you frequently buy books that you don't actually read.

With any luck, this journal will enrich your reading experience, help you discover new favorites, and make you an even more curious reader than you already were. And maybe it will even motivate you to tackle that to-be-read pile, too.

My Top 10 Titles for 20___

1
WHY:

2
WHY:

3
WHY:

4
WHY:

5
WHY:

6
WHY:

7
WHY:

8
WHY:

9
WHY:

10
WHY:

FAMOUS AUTHORS' FAVORITE BOOKS

GEORGE R.R. MARTIN (*A Game of Thrones*) has not surprisingly said that J.R.R. Tolkien's *The Lord of the Rings*, which he first read in junior high, is "still a book I admire vastly."

JOAN DIDION In an interview with *The Paris Review* in 2006, novelist and creative nonfiction scribe Joan Didion called Joseph Conrad's *Victory* "maybe my favorite book in the world . . . I have never started a novel . . . without rereading *Victory*. It opens up the possibilities of a novel. It makes it seem worth doing."

MEG WOLITZER (*The Interestings*) told *Elle,* "I can't say I've read anything else like [Jane Gardam's] *Old Filth*, which stands out for me as a singular, opalescent novel, a thing of beauty that gives immense gratification to its lucky readers."

ERIK LARSON (*The Devil in the White City*) calls Dashiell Hammett's *The Maltese Falcon* his "all-time personal favorite."

EDWIDGE DANTICAT This MacArthur Fellow and award-winning author of *Claire of the Sea Light*, *The Dew Breaker*, and *Brother, I'm Dying* told Time.com that her favorite summer read is *Love, Anger, Madness* by the Haitian writer Marie Vieux-Chauvet. "I have read and reread that book, both in French and in its English translation, for many years now," she said. "And each time I stumble into something new and eye-opening that makes me want to keep reading it over and over again."

THE ORIGINS OF 4 FAMOUS AUTHORS' PEN NAMES

GEORGE ORWELL

Just before publishing his first novel, Eric Arthur Blair decided to write under a pen name to avoid embarrassing his family. He took the first name from the patron saint of England and the reigning monarch in the first half of the 1930s, and the last name from the River Orwell, a popular sailing spot, which he loved to visit.

TONI MORRISON

Born Chloe Wofford, Morrison began going by Toni—an abbreviation of her baptismal name, Anthony—when she went to Howard University. "The people in Washington, they don't know how to pronounce C-H-L-O-E," she told NPR. Someone called her Toni, and she went with it, saying, "It's easy. You don't have to mispronounce my name." When she got married in 1958, she took her husband Harold Morrison's last name, and though they divorced in 1964, she used Morrison on her first novel, 1970's *The Bluest Eye*. She tried to get it changed back to her maiden name before publication but was told it was too late. In a 2012 *New York* magazine profile, Morrison said it was something she regretted: "Wasn't that stupid? I feel ruined!"

AYN RAND

Born Alissa Zinovievna Rosenbaum in St. Petersburg, Russia, the future *Atlas Shrugged* author changed her name when she immigrated to the US in 1926. Though legend has it that she got her last name from a Remington Rand typewriter, Rand was probably an abbreviation of Rosenbaum. According to the author, Ayn was a variant of a Finnish name, but some believe it was actually derived from the childhood nickname Ayin; others believe the name may have had meaning to her that we'll never know.

JOHN LE CARRÉ

The author of spy novels was *himself* a spy in England when he began publishing novels in 1961. His employers had no issues with his writing novels, but they said he'd have to use a pseudonym. His publisher suggested that David John Moore Cornwell go by something like Chuck Smith. But as for how he came up with John le Carré, well . . . he couldn't remember. "I was asked so many times why I chose this ridiculous name, then the writer's imagination came to my help," the author told *The Paris Review*. "I saw myself riding over Battersea Bridge, on top of a bus, looking down at a tailor's shop . . . And it *was* called something of this sort—*le Carré*. That satisfied everybody for years. But lies don't last with age. I find a frightful compulsion toward truth these days. And the truth is, I don't know."

If I Wrote a Book,
My Pen Name Would Be

....

3 AUTHORS I WOULD INVITE TO A

Literary Dinner Party

1 _____
WHY: _____
_____
_____

2 _____
WHY: _____
_____

3 _____
WHY: _____
_____
_____

THE DISHES 5 WRITERS WOULD BRING TO A LITERARY POTLUCK

PEARL S. BUCK:
Sweet and Sour Fish
Buck grew up in China, which she used as the basis of her Pulitzer Prize–winning *The Good Earth*. As a child, she had meals with Chinese servants instead of eating American fare with her family, an experience that inspired her to write the *Oriental Cookbook* in 1972.

HARPER LEE:
Crackling Bread
If you had asked the Pulitzer Prize–winning author of *To Kill a Mockingbird* why the South lost the Civil War, she might have blamed the soldiers' hankering for crackling bread, a mix of cornmeal and crispy-fried pork skins. "Some historians say this recipe alone fell the Confederacy," Lee wrote. Understandable, considering her recipe begins: "First, catch your pig."

JOHN STEINBECK:
Posole
Steinbeck liked to eat local. In England, he'd hunt for dandelion greens. In California, he made butter and cheese with the milk from his own personal cow. In New York, he fished for dinner. But traveling on the road, Steinbeck ate like a college freshman. His posole recipe is simply a "can of chile and a can of hominy."

MARCEL PROUST:
Madeleines
In the most pivotal scene in Proust's *In Search of Lost Time*, the narrator soaks a madeleine cake in his cup of tea, takes a bite, and is instantly overcome with nostalgia for his childhood. In early versions of Proust's seminal work, the tiny treat began as much less poetic fare—toasted bread.

SYLVIA PLATH:
Tomato Soup Cake
Plath often wrote as she baked—in fact, she penned "Death & Co." while she made her specialty, tomato soup cake.

JHUMPA LAHIRI came up with the phrase that would become the title of her Pulitzer Prize–winning first book, *Interpreter of Maladies*, during graduate school. She ran into an acquaintance who was working in a doctor's office, serving as a translator between the doctor and his patients. "The phrase 'interpreter of maladies' popped into my head as a way of describing what this person was doing," she recalled. "It lingered long enough for me to jot the phrase down."

What's in a Name?

Polish author OLGA TOKARCZUK borrowed the title of her novel *Drive Your Plow Over the Bones of the Dead* from William Blake's poem "Proverbs of Hell." "I came up with the title thinking about the old Polish detective stories, like Joe Alex, where the titles were sometimes taken from a verse, or a poem, or a nursery rhyme. Agatha Christie did it, too," she explained during an interview at the Brooklyn Public Library in 2010. The publishers pushed back, thinking the title was too wordy to attract readers, but Tokarczuk ultimately won out. She also eventually won something else: the Nobel Prize in Literature.

BOOK TITLES

I LOVE

_____

_____

THE *Title* FOR MY

AUTOBIOGRAPHY WOULD BE

10

NOVELS MOST OFTEN ABANDONED BY READERS

Just because you buy or borrow a book doesn't necessarily mean that you'll actually finish—or even start—reading it. Though tracking which books don't get finished is not an exact science, people have tried to figure it out; Goodreads, for example, has created a virtual shelf for members to leave their abandoned books. Since there are millions of people who *don't* report their reading habits on Goodreads, you shouldn't take any of these statistics too seriously. However, here's a list of 10 books Goodreads users gave up on:

1. *The Casual Vacancy* by J.K. Rowling
2. *Catch-22* by Joseph Heller
3. *American Gods* by Neil Gaiman
4. *A Game of Thrones* by George R.R. Martin
5. *The Goldfinch* by Donna Tartt
6. *The Book Thief* by Markus Zusak
7. *Outlander* by Diana Gabaldon
8. *One Hundred Years of Solitude* by Gabriel García Márquez
9. *Infinite Jest* by David Foster Wallace
10. *Fifty Shades of Grey* by E.L. James

3 Classic Books I Couldn't Finish

1 _____

WHY: _____

_____

_____

2 _____

WHY: _____

_____

_____

3 _____

WHY: _____

_____

_____

"I have just finished a book which is an unforgettable experience in reading," First Lady Eleanor Roosevelt wrote in the column My Day in 1939. "*Grapes of Wrath* by John Steinbeck, both repels and attracts you. The horrors of the picture, so well-drawn, made you dread sometimes to begin the next chapter, and yet you cannot lay the book down or even skip a page . . . the book is coarse in spots, but life is coarse in spots, [and the] story is very beautiful in spots just as life is." The book won the Pulitzer Prize in 1940.

5 CAT-LOVING WRITERS

Some of history's most successful writers were devoted to their furry friends, including these five.

THE BRONTË SISTERS

Many of the Brontë sisters' published works featured felines, and cats make appearances in Anne and Charlotte's diaries as well. In 1842, while living in Brussels, Emily wrote an essay in French called "Le Chat" ("The Cat") that defended cats against people who say they're cruel—and made points about human nature while she was at it. The sisters didn't just write about cats, either; at their home in Haworth, England, they had a black cat named Tom and a tabby named Tiger.

WILLIAM S. BURROUGHS

William S. Burroughs is known for his wild, drug-induced writings, but he had a softer side as well—especially when it came to his cats. He penned an autobiographical novella, *The Cat Inside,* about the felines he adopted throughout his life, and the final journal entry Burroughs wrote before he died referred to the pure love he had for his four pets: "Only thing can resolve conflict is love, like I felt for Fletch and Ruski, Spooner, and Calico. Pure love. What I feel for my cats present and past."

MARK TWAIN

When his beloved black cat Bambino went missing, Mark Twain took out an advertisement in the *New York American* offering a $5 reward to return the missing cat to his house at 21 Fifth Avenue in New York City. It described Bambino as "Large and intensely black; thick, velvety fur; has a faint fringe of white hair across his chest; not easy to find in ordinary light." (For the record, Bambino made it back just fine.)

PATRICIA HIGHSMITH

Patricia Highsmith once said, "My imagination functions better when I don't have to speak with people," but she did virtually everything with her cats: She wrote next to them, she ate next to them, and she even slept next to them. She kept them by her side throughout her life until her death at her home in Locarno, Switzerland, in 1995.

CHARLES DICKENS

Charles Dickens had a soft spot for a few felines in his life. In 1862, he was so upset after the death of his favorite cat, Bob, that he had the kitty's paw stuffed and mounted to an ivory letter opener. He had the opener engraved saying, "C.D., In memory of Bob, 1862" so he could have a constant reminder of his old friend.

MY FAVORITE ANIMAL IN A BOOK IS

Parts of *The Art of Racing in the Rain* by Garth Stein were inspired by real life. Stein used to be a race car driver; he stopped racing after he got into an accident, incidentally, while it was raining. According to Stein's website, Enzo—the dog narrating the story—is based on an Airedale Terrier his family owned when he was a child.

REPORT CARD

Kurt Vonnegut graded his books: *Cat's Cradle* and *Slaughterhouse-Five* both got an A+, while *Slapstick* got a D.

THE GRADE I'D GIVE THE LAST 3 BOOKS I'VE READ

TITLE: _____

GRADE: ☐ A+ ☐ A ☐ A- ☐ B+ ☐ B ☐ B- ☐ C+ ☐ C ☐ C- ☐ D+ ☐ D ☐ D- ☐ F

WHY: _____

TITLE: _____

GRADE: ☐ A+ ☐ A ☐ A- ☐ B+ ☐ B ☐ B- ☐ C+ ☐ C ☐ C- ☐ D+ ☐ D ☐ D- ☐ F

WHY: _____

TITLE: _____

GRADE: ☐ A+ ☐ A ☐ A- ☐ B+ ☐ B ☐ B- ☐ C+ ☐ C ☐ C- ☐ D+ ☐ D ☐ D- ☐ F

WHY: _____

TITLE: _____

AUTHOR: _____

DATE READ: _____

THOUGHTS: _____

_____

_____

_____

RATINGS

CHARACTERS
☆ ☆ ☆ ☆ ☆

PLOT DEVELOPMENT
☆ ☆ ☆ ☆ ☆

QUALITY OF WRITING
☆ ☆ ☆ ☆ ☆

OVERALL
☆ ☆ ☆ ☆ ☆

TITLE: _____

AUTHOR: _____

DATE READ: _____

THOUGHTS: _____

_____

_____

_____

RATINGS

CHARACTERS
☆ ☆ ☆ ☆ ☆

PLOT DEVELOPMENT
☆ ☆ ☆ ☆ ☆

QUALITY OF WRITING
☆ ☆ ☆ ☆ ☆

OVERALL
☆ ☆ ☆ ☆ ☆

TITLE: _____

AUTHOR: _____

DATE READ: _____

THOUGHTS: _____

_____

_____

_____

RATINGS

CHARACTERS
☆ ☆ ☆ ☆ ☆

PLOT DEVELOPMENT
☆ ☆ ☆ ☆ ☆

QUALITY OF WRITING
☆ ☆ ☆ ☆ ☆

OVERALL
☆ ☆ ☆ ☆ ☆

TITLE: _____

AUTHOR: _____

DATE READ: _____

THOUGHTS: _____

_____

_____

_____

RATINGS

CHARACTERS
☆ ☆ ☆ ☆ ☆

PLOT DEVELOPMENT
☆ ☆ ☆ ☆ ☆

QUALITY OF WRITING
☆ ☆ ☆ ☆ ☆

OVERALL
☆ ☆ ☆ ☆ ☆

BOOKS I'VE READ

TITLE: _____

AUTHOR: _____

DATE READ: _____

THOUGHTS: _____

_____

_____

_____

RATINGS

CHARACTERS

☆ ☆ ☆ ☆ ☆

PLOT DEVELOPMENT

☆ ☆ ☆ ☆ ☆

QUALITY OF WRITING

☆ ☆ ☆ ☆ ☆

OVERALL

☆ ☆ ☆ ☆ ☆

TITLE: _____

AUTHOR: _____

DATE READ: _____

THOUGHTS: _____

_____

_____

_____

RATINGS

CHARACTERS

☆ ☆ ☆ ☆ ☆

PLOT DEVELOPMENT

☆ ☆ ☆ ☆ ☆

QUALITY OF WRITING

☆ ☆ ☆ ☆ ☆

OVERALL

☆ ☆ ☆ ☆ ☆

TITLE: _____

AUTHOR: _____

DATE READ: _____

THOUGHTS: _____

_____

_____

_____

RATINGS

CHARACTERS

☆ ☆ ☆ ☆ ☆

PLOT DEVELOPMENT

☆ ☆ ☆ ☆ ☆

QUALITY OF WRITING

☆ ☆ ☆ ☆ ☆

OVERALL

☆ ☆ ☆ ☆ ☆

TITLE: _____

AUTHOR: _____

DATE READ: _____

THOUGHTS: _____

_____

_____

_____

RATINGS

CHARACTERS

☆ ☆ ☆ ☆ ☆

PLOT DEVELOPMENT

☆ ☆ ☆ ☆ ☆

QUALITY OF WRITING

☆ ☆ ☆ ☆ ☆

OVERALL

☆ ☆ ☆ ☆ ☆

TITLE: _____

AUTHOR: _____

DATE READ: _____

THOUGHTS: _____

_____

_____

_____

RATINGS

CHARACTERS
☆ ☆ ☆ ☆ ☆

PLOT DEVELOPMENT
☆ ☆ ☆ ☆ ☆

QUALITY OF WRITING
☆ ☆ ☆ ☆ ☆

OVERALL
☆ ☆ ☆ ☆ ☆

TITLE: _____

AUTHOR: _____

DATE READ: _____

THOUGHTS: _____

_____

_____

_____

RATINGS

CHARACTERS
☆ ☆ ☆ ☆ ☆

PLOT DEVELOPMENT
☆ ☆ ☆ ☆ ☆

QUALITY OF WRITING
☆ ☆ ☆ ☆ ☆

OVERALL
☆ ☆ ☆ ☆ ☆

TITLE: _____

AUTHOR: _____

DATE READ: _____

THOUGHTS: _____

_____

_____

_____

RATINGS

CHARACTERS
☆ ☆ ☆ ☆ ☆

PLOT DEVELOPMENT
☆ ☆ ☆ ☆ ☆

QUALITY OF WRITING
☆ ☆ ☆ ☆ ☆

OVERALL
☆ ☆ ☆ ☆ ☆

"**You can never get a cup of tea large enough or a book long enough to suit me.**" —C.S. LEWIS

BOOKS I'VE READ

TITLE: _____

AUTHOR: _____

DATE READ: _____

THOUGHTS: _____

_____

_____

_____

RATINGS

CHARACTERS
☆ ☆ ☆ ☆ ☆

PLOT DEVELOPMENT
☆ ☆ ☆ ☆ ☆

QUALITY OF WRITING
☆ ☆ ☆ ☆ ☆

OVERALL
☆ ☆ ☆ ☆ ☆

TITLE: _____

AUTHOR: _____

DATE READ: _____

THOUGHTS: _____

_____

_____

_____

RATINGS

CHARACTERS
☆ ☆ ☆ ☆ ☆

PLOT DEVELOPMENT
☆ ☆ ☆ ☆ ☆

QUALITY OF WRITING
☆ ☆ ☆ ☆ ☆

OVERALL
☆ ☆ ☆ ☆ ☆

TITLE: _____

AUTHOR: _____

DATE READ: _____

THOUGHTS: _____

_____

_____

_____

RATINGS

CHARACTERS
☆ ☆ ☆ ☆ ☆

PLOT DEVELOPMENT
☆ ☆ ☆ ☆ ☆

QUALITY OF WRITING
☆ ☆ ☆ ☆ ☆

OVERALL
☆ ☆ ☆ ☆ ☆

TITLE: _____

AUTHOR: _____

DATE READ: _____

THOUGHTS: _____

_____

_____

_____

RATINGS

CHARACTERS
☆ ☆ ☆ ☆ ☆

PLOT DEVELOPMENT
☆ ☆ ☆ ☆ ☆

QUALITY OF WRITING
☆ ☆ ☆ ☆ ☆

OVERALL
☆ ☆ ☆ ☆ ☆

TITLE: _____

AUTHOR: _____

DATE READ: _____

THOUGHTS: _____

_____

_____

_____

RATINGS

CHARACTERS

☆ ☆ ☆ ☆ ☆

PLOT DEVELOPMENT

☆ ☆ ☆ ☆ ☆

QUALITY OF WRITING

☆ ☆ ☆ ☆ ☆

OVERALL

☆ ☆ ☆ ☆ ☆

TITLE: _____

AUTHOR: _____

DATE READ: _____

THOUGHTS: _____

_____

_____

_____

RATINGS

CHARACTERS

☆ ☆ ☆ ☆ ☆

PLOT DEVELOPMENT

☆ ☆ ☆ ☆ ☆

QUALITY OF WRITING

☆ ☆ ☆ ☆ ☆

OVERALL

☆ ☆ ☆ ☆ ☆

TITLE: _____

AUTHOR: _____

DATE READ: _____

THOUGHTS: _____

_____

_____

_____

RATINGS

CHARACTERS

☆ ☆ ☆ ☆ ☆

PLOT DEVELOPMENT

☆ ☆ ☆ ☆ ☆

QUALITY OF WRITING

☆ ☆ ☆ ☆ ☆

OVERALL

☆ ☆ ☆ ☆ ☆

TITLE: _____

AUTHOR: _____

DATE READ: _____

THOUGHTS: _____

_____

_____

_____

RATINGS

CHARACTERS

☆ ☆ ☆ ☆ ☆

PLOT DEVELOPMENT

☆ ☆ ☆ ☆ ☆

QUALITY OF WRITING

☆ ☆ ☆ ☆ ☆

OVERALL

☆ ☆ ☆ ☆ ☆

TITLE: _____

AUTHOR: _____

DATE READ: _____

THOUGHTS: _____

_____

_____

_____

RATINGS

CHARACTERS
☆ ☆ ☆ ☆ ☆

PLOT DEVELOPMENT
☆ ☆ ☆ ☆ ☆

QUALITY OF WRITING
☆ ☆ ☆ ☆ ☆

OVERALL
☆ ☆ ☆ ☆ ☆

TITLE: _____

AUTHOR: _____

DATE READ: _____

THOUGHTS: _____

_____

_____

_____

RATINGS

CHARACTERS
☆ ☆ ☆ ☆ ☆

PLOT DEVELOPMENT
☆ ☆ ☆ ☆ ☆

QUALITY OF WRITING
☆ ☆ ☆ ☆ ☆

OVERALL
☆ ☆ ☆ ☆ ☆

> **"That is part of the beauty of all literature. You discover that your longings are universal longings, that you're not lonely and isolated from anyone. You belong."**
>
> —F. SCOTT FITZGERALD, to Sheilah Graham

TITLE: _____

AUTHOR: _____

DATE READ: _____

THOUGHTS: _____

_____

_____

_____

RATINGS

CHARACTERS
☆ ☆ ☆ ☆ ☆

PLOT DEVELOPMENT
☆ ☆ ☆ ☆ ☆

QUALITY OF WRITING
☆ ☆ ☆ ☆ ☆

OVERALL
☆ ☆ ☆ ☆ ☆

TITLE: _____

AUTHOR: _____

DATE READ: _____

THOUGHTS: _____

_____

_____

_____

RATINGS

CHARACTERS
☆ ☆ ☆ ☆ ☆

PLOT DEVELOPMENT
☆ ☆ ☆ ☆ ☆

QUALITY OF WRITING
☆ ☆ ☆ ☆ ☆

OVERALL
☆ ☆ ☆ ☆ ☆

TITLE: _____

AUTHOR: _____

DATE READ: _____

THOUGHTS: _____

_____

_____

_____

RATINGS

CHARACTERS
☆ ☆ ☆ ☆ ☆

PLOT DEVELOPMENT
☆ ☆ ☆ ☆ ☆

QUALITY OF WRITING
☆ ☆ ☆ ☆ ☆

OVERALL
☆ ☆ ☆ ☆ ☆

TITLE: _____

AUTHOR: _____

DATE READ: _____

THOUGHTS: _____

_____

_____

_____

RATINGS

CHARACTERS
☆ ☆ ☆ ☆ ☆

PLOT DEVELOPMENT
☆ ☆ ☆ ☆ ☆

QUALITY OF WRITING
☆ ☆ ☆ ☆ ☆

OVERALL
☆ ☆ ☆ ☆ ☆

TITLE: _____

AUTHOR: _____

DATE READ: _____

THOUGHTS: _____

_____

_____

_____

RATINGS

CHARACTERS
☆ ☆ ☆ ☆ ☆

PLOT DEVELOPMENT
☆ ☆ ☆ ☆ ☆

QUALITY OF WRITING
☆ ☆ ☆ ☆ ☆

OVERALL
☆ ☆ ☆ ☆ ☆

TITLE: _____

AUTHOR: _____

DATE READ: _____

THOUGHTS: _____

_____

_____

_____

RATINGS

CHARACTERS
☆ ☆ ☆ ☆ ☆

PLOT DEVELOPMENT
☆ ☆ ☆ ☆ ☆

QUALITY OF WRITING
☆ ☆ ☆ ☆ ☆

OVERALL
☆ ☆ ☆ ☆ ☆

TITLE: _____

AUTHOR: _____

DATE READ: _____

THOUGHTS: _____

_____

_____

_____

RATINGS

CHARACTERS
☆ ☆ ☆ ☆ ☆

PLOT DEVELOPMENT
☆ ☆ ☆ ☆ ☆

QUALITY OF WRITING
☆ ☆ ☆ ☆ ☆

OVERALL
☆ ☆ ☆ ☆ ☆

TITLE: _____

AUTHOR: _____

DATE READ: _____

THOUGHTS: _____

_____

_____

_____

RATINGS

CHARACTERS
☆ ☆ ☆ ☆ ☆

PLOT DEVELOPMENT
☆ ☆ ☆ ☆ ☆

QUALITY OF WRITING
☆ ☆ ☆ ☆ ☆

OVERALL
☆ ☆ ☆ ☆ ☆

TITLE: _____

AUTHOR: _____

DATE READ: _____

THOUGHTS: _____

_____

_____

_____

RATINGS

CHARACTERS
☆ ☆ ☆ ☆ ☆

PLOT DEVELOPMENT
☆ ☆ ☆ ☆ ☆

QUALITY OF WRITING
☆ ☆ ☆ ☆ ☆

OVERALL
☆ ☆ ☆ ☆ ☆

TITLE: _____

AUTHOR: _____

DATE READ: _____

THOUGHTS: _____

_____

_____

_____

RATINGS

CHARACTERS

☆ ☆ ☆ ☆ ☆

PLOT DEVELOPMENT

☆ ☆ ☆ ☆ ☆

QUALITY OF WRITING

☆ ☆ ☆ ☆ ☆

OVERALL

☆ ☆ ☆ ☆ ☆

TITLE: _____

AUTHOR: _____

DATE READ: _____

THOUGHTS: _____

_____

_____

_____

RATINGS

CHARACTERS

☆ ☆ ☆ ☆ ☆

PLOT DEVELOPMENT

☆ ☆ ☆ ☆ ☆

QUALITY OF WRITING

☆ ☆ ☆ ☆ ☆

OVERALL

☆ ☆ ☆ ☆ ☆

TITLE: _____

AUTHOR: _____

DATE READ: _____

THOUGHTS: _____

_____

_____

_____

RATINGS

CHARACTERS

☆ ☆ ☆ ☆ ☆

PLOT DEVELOPMENT

☆ ☆ ☆ ☆ ☆

QUALITY OF WRITING

☆ ☆ ☆ ☆ ☆

OVERALL

☆ ☆ ☆ ☆ ☆

TITLE: _____

AUTHOR: _____

DATE READ: _____

THOUGHTS: _____

_____

_____

_____

RATINGS

CHARACTERS

☆ ☆ ☆ ☆ ☆

PLOT DEVELOPMENT

☆ ☆ ☆ ☆ ☆

QUALITY OF WRITING

☆ ☆ ☆ ☆ ☆

OVERALL

☆ ☆ ☆ ☆

TITLE: _____

AUTHOR: _____

DATE READ: _____

THOUGHTS: _____

_____

_____

_____

RATINGS

CHARACTERS

☆ ☆ ☆ ☆ ☆

PLOT DEVELOPMENT

☆ ☆ ☆ ☆ ☆

QUALITY OF WRITING

☆ ☆ ☆ ☆ ☆

OVERALL

☆ ☆ ☆ ☆ ☆

TITLE: _____

AUTHOR: _____

DATE READ: _____

THOUGHTS: _____

_____

_____

_____

RATINGS

CHARACTERS

☆ ☆ ☆ ☆ ☆

PLOT DEVELOPMENT

☆ ☆ ☆ ☆ ☆

QUALITY OF WRITING

☆ ☆ ☆ ☆ ☆

OVERALL

☆ ☆ ☆ ☆ ☆

TITLE: _____

AUTHOR: _____

DATE READ: _____

THOUGHTS: _____

_____

_____

_____

RATINGS

CHARACTERS

☆ ☆ ☆ ☆ ☆

PLOT DEVELOPMENT

☆ ☆ ☆ ☆ ☆

QUALITY OF WRITING

☆ ☆ ☆ ☆ ☆

OVERALL

☆ ☆ ☆ ☆ ☆

TITLE: _____

AUTHOR: _____

DATE READ: _____

THOUGHTS: _____

_____

_____

_____

RATINGS

CHARACTERS

☆ ☆ ☆ ☆ ☆

PLOT DEVELOPMENT

☆ ☆ ☆ ☆ ☆

QUALITY OF WRITING

☆ ☆ ☆ ☆ ☆

OVERALL

☆ ☆ ☆ ☆ ☆

TITLE: _____

AUTHOR: _____

DATE READ: _____

THOUGHTS: _____

_____

_____

_____

RATINGS

CHARACTERS
☆ ☆ ☆ ☆ ☆

PLOT DEVELOPMENT
☆ ☆ ☆ ☆ ☆

QUALITY OF WRITING
☆ ☆ ☆ ☆ ☆

OVERALL
☆ ☆ ☆ ☆ ☆

"My life is a reading list."

—JOHN IRVING, *A Prayer for Owen Meany*

TITLE: _____

AUTHOR: _____

DATE READ: _____

THOUGHTS: _____

_____

_____

_____

RATINGS

CHARACTERS
☆ ☆ ☆ ☆ ☆

PLOT DEVELOPMENT
☆ ☆ ☆ ☆ ☆

QUALITY OF WRITING
☆ ☆ ☆ ☆ ☆

OVERALL
☆ ☆ ☆ ☆ ☆

TITLE: _____

AUTHOR: _____

DATE READ: _____

THOUGHTS: _____

_____

_____

_____

RATINGS

CHARACTERS
☆ ☆ ☆ ☆ ☆

PLOT DEVELOPMENT
☆ ☆ ☆ ☆ ☆

QUALITY OF WRITING
☆ ☆ ☆ ☆ ☆

OVERALL
☆ ☆ ☆ ☆ ☆

BOOKS I'VE READ

TITLE: _____

AUTHOR: _____

DATE READ: _____

THOUGHTS: _____

_____

_____

_____

RATINGS

CHARACTERS
☆ ☆ ☆ ☆ ☆

PLOT DEVELOPMENT
☆ ☆ ☆ ☆ ☆

QUALITY OF WRITING
☆ ☆ ☆ ☆ ☆

OVERALL
☆ ☆ ☆ ☆ ☆

TITLE: _____

AUTHOR: _____

DATE READ: _____

THOUGHTS: _____

_____

_____

_____

RATINGS

CHARACTERS
☆ ☆ ☆ ☆ ☆

PLOT DEVELOPMENT
☆ ☆ ☆ ☆ ☆

QUALITY OF WRITING
☆ ☆ ☆ ☆ ☆

OVERALL
☆ ☆ ☆ ☆ ☆

TITLE: _____

AUTHOR: _____

DATE READ: _____

THOUGHTS: _____

_____

_____

_____

RATINGS

CHARACTERS
☆ ☆ ☆ ☆ ☆

PLOT DEVELOPMENT
☆ ☆ ☆ ☆ ☆

QUALITY OF WRITING
☆ ☆ ☆ ☆ ☆

OVERALL
☆ ☆ ☆ ☆ ☆

TITLE: _____

AUTHOR: _____

DATE READ: _____

THOUGHTS: _____

_____

_____

_____

RATINGS

CHARACTERS
☆ ☆ ☆ ☆ ☆

PLOT DEVELOPMENT
☆ ☆ ☆ ☆ ☆

QUALITY OF WRITING
☆ ☆ ☆ ☆ ☆

OVERALL
☆ ☆ ☆ ☆ ☆

TITLE: _____

AUTHOR: _____

DATE READ: _____

THOUGHTS: _____

_____

_____

_____

RATINGS

CHARACTERS
☆ ☆ ☆ ☆ ☆

PLOT DEVELOPMENT
☆ ☆ ☆ ☆ ☆

QUALITY OF WRITING
☆ ☆ ☆ ☆ ☆

OVERALL
☆ ☆ ☆ ☆ ☆

TITLE: _____

AUTHOR: _____

DATE READ: _____

THOUGHTS: _____

_____

_____

_____

RATINGS

CHARACTERS
☆ ☆ ☆ ☆ ☆

PLOT DEVELOPMENT
☆ ☆ ☆ ☆ ☆

QUALITY OF WRITING
☆ ☆ ☆ ☆ ☆

OVERALL
☆ ☆ ☆ ☆ ☆

TITLE: _____

AUTHOR: _____

DATE READ: _____

THOUGHTS: _____

_____

_____

_____

RATINGS

CHARACTERS
☆ ☆ ☆ ☆ ☆

PLOT DEVELOPMENT
☆ ☆ ☆ ☆ ☆

QUALITY OF WRITING
☆ ☆ ☆ ☆ ☆

OVERALL
☆ ☆ ☆ ☆ ☆

"**Sometimes, you read a book and it fills you with this weird evangelical zeal, and you become convinced that the shattered world will never be put back together unless and until all living humans read the book.**"

—**JOHN GREEN,** *The Fault in Our Stars*

BOOKS I'VE READ

TITLE: _____

AUTHOR: _____

DATE READ: _____

THOUGHTS: _____

_____

_____

_____

RATINGS

CHARACTERS

☆ ☆ ☆ ☆ ☆

PLOT DEVELOPMENT

☆ ☆ ☆ ☆ ☆

QUALITY OF WRITING

☆ ☆ ☆ ☆ ☆

OVERALL

☆ ☆ ☆ ☆ ☆

TITLE: _____

AUTHOR: _____

DATE READ: _____

THOUGHTS: _____

_____

_____

_____

RATINGS

CHARACTERS

☆ ☆ ☆ ☆ ☆

PLOT DEVELOPMENT

☆ ☆ ☆ ☆ ☆

QUALITY OF WRITING

☆ ☆ ☆ ☆ ☆

OVERALL

☆ ☆ ☆ ☆ ☆

TITLE: _____

AUTHOR: _____

DATE READ: _____

THOUGHTS: _____

_____

_____

_____

RATINGS

CHARACTERS

☆ ☆ ☆ ☆ ☆

PLOT DEVELOPMENT

☆ ☆ ☆ ☆ ☆

QUALITY OF WRITING

☆ ☆ ☆ ☆ ☆

OVERALL

☆ ☆ ☆ ☆ ☆

TITLE: _____

AUTHOR: _____

DATE READ: _____

THOUGHTS: _____

_____

_____

_____

RATINGS

CHARACTERS

☆ ☆ ☆ ☆ ☆

PLOT DEVELOPMENT

☆ ☆ ☆ ☆ ☆

QUALITY OF WRITING

☆ ☆ ☆ ☆ ☆

OVERALL

☆ ☆ ☆ ☆ ☆

TITLE: _____

AUTHOR: _____

DATE READ: _____

THOUGHTS: _____

_____

_____

_____

_____

RATINGS

CHARACTERS

☆ ☆ ☆ ☆ ☆

PLOT DEVELOPMENT

☆ ☆ ☆ ☆ ☆

QUALITY OF WRITING

☆ ☆ ☆ ☆ ☆

OVERALL

☆ ☆ ☆ ☆ ☆

TITLE: _____

AUTHOR: _____

DATE READ: _____

THOUGHTS: _____

_____

_____

_____

_____

RATINGS

CHARACTERS

☆ ☆ ☆ ☆ ☆

PLOT DEVELOPMENT

☆ ☆ ☆ ☆ ☆

QUALITY OF WRITING

☆ ☆ ☆ ☆ ☆

OVERALL

☆ ☆ ☆ ☆ ☆

TITLE: _____

AUTHOR: _____

DATE READ: _____

THOUGHTS: _____

_____

_____

_____

_____

RATINGS

CHARACTERS

☆ ☆ ☆ ☆ ☆

PLOT DEVELOPMENT

☆ ☆ ☆ ☆ ☆

QUALITY OF WRITING

☆ ☆ ☆ ☆ ☆

OVERALL

☆ ☆ ☆ ☆ ☆

TITLE: _____

AUTHOR: _____

DATE READ: _____

THOUGHTS: _____

_____

_____

_____

_____

RATINGS

CHARACTERS

☆ ☆ ☆ ☆ ☆

PLOT DEVELOPMENT

☆ ☆ ☆ ☆ ☆

QUALITY OF WRITING

☆ ☆ ☆ ☆ ☆

OVERALL

☆ ☆ ☆ ☆ ☆

BOOKS I'VE READ

TITLE: _____
AUTHOR: _____
DATE READ: _____
THOUGHTS: _____
_____
_____
_____

RATINGS

CHARACTERS
☆ ☆ ☆ ☆ ☆

PLOT DEVELOPMENT
☆ ☆ ☆ ☆ ☆

QUALITY OF WRITING
☆ ☆ ☆ ☆ ☆

OVERALL
☆ ☆ ☆ ☆ ☆

TITLE: _____
AUTHOR: _____
DATE READ: _____
THOUGHTS: _____
_____
_____
_____

RATINGS

CHARACTERS
☆ ☆ ☆ ☆ ☆

PLOT DEVELOPMENT
☆ ☆ ☆ ☆ ☆

QUALITY OF WRITING
☆ ☆ ☆ ☆ ☆

OVERALL
☆ ☆ ☆ ☆ ☆

TITLE: _____
AUTHOR: _____
DATE READ: _____
THOUGHTS: _____
_____
_____
_____

RATINGS

CHARACTERS
☆ ☆ ☆ ☆ ☆

PLOT DEVELOPMENT
☆ ☆ ☆ ☆ ☆

QUALITY OF WRITING
☆ ☆ ☆ ☆ ☆

OVERALL
☆ ☆ ☆ ☆ ☆

TITLE: _____
AUTHOR: _____
DATE READ: _____
THOUGHTS: _____
_____
_____
_____

RATINGS

CHARACTERS
☆ ☆ ☆ ☆ ☆

PLOT DEVELOPMENT
☆ ☆ ☆ ☆ ☆

QUALITY OF WRITING
☆ ☆ ☆ ☆ ☆

OVERALL
☆ ☆ ☆ ☆ ☆

TITLE: _____

AUTHOR: _____

DATE READ: _____

THOUGHTS: _____

_____

_____

_____

RATINGS

CHARACTERS
☆ ☆ ☆ ☆ ☆

PLOT DEVELOPMENT
☆ ☆ ☆ ☆ ☆

QUALITY OF WRITING
☆ ☆ ☆ ☆ ☆

OVERALL
☆ ☆ ☆ ☆ ☆

TITLE: _____

AUTHOR: _____

DATE READ: _____

THOUGHTS: _____

_____

_____

_____

RATINGS

CHARACTERS
☆ ☆ ☆ ☆ ☆

PLOT DEVELOPMENT
☆ ☆ ☆ ☆ ☆

QUALITY OF WRITING
☆ ☆ ☆ ☆ ☆

OVERALL
☆ ☆ ☆ ☆ ☆

TITLE: _____

AUTHOR: _____

DATE READ: _____

THOUGHTS: _____

_____

_____

_____

RATINGS

CHARACTERS
☆ ☆ ☆ ☆ ☆

PLOT DEVELOPMENT
☆ ☆ ☆ ☆ ☆

QUALITY OF WRITING
☆ ☆ ☆ ☆ ☆

OVERALL
☆ ☆ ☆ ☆ ☆

> **"There is no such thing as a moral or immoral book. Books are well written or badly written. That is all."**
>
> —OSCAR WILDE, _The Picture of Dorian Gray_

BOOKS I'VE READ

TITLE: _____

AUTHOR: _____

DATE READ: _____

THOUGHTS: _____

_____

_____

_____

RATINGS

CHARACTERS

☆ ☆ ☆ ☆ ☆

PLOT DEVELOPMENT

☆ ☆ ☆ ☆ ☆

QUALITY OF WRITING

☆ ☆ ☆ ☆ ☆

OVERALL

☆ ☆ ☆ ☆ ☆

TITLE: _____

AUTHOR: _____

DATE READ: _____

THOUGHTS: _____

_____

_____

_____

RATINGS

CHARACTERS

☆ ☆ ☆ ☆ ☆

PLOT DEVELOPMENT

☆ ☆ ☆ ☆ ☆

QUALITY OF WRITING

☆ ☆ ☆ ☆ ☆

OVERALL

☆ ☆ ☆ ☆ ☆

TITLE: _____

AUTHOR: _____

DATE READ: _____

THOUGHTS: _____

_____

_____

_____

RATINGS

CHARACTERS

☆ ☆ ☆ ☆ ☆

PLOT DEVELOPMENT

☆ ☆ ☆ ☆ ☆

QUALITY OF WRITING

☆ ☆ ☆ ☆ ☆

OVERALL

☆ ☆ ☆ ☆ ☆

TITLE: _____

AUTHOR: _____

DATE READ: _____

THOUGHTS: _____

_____

_____

_____

RATINGS

CHARACTERS

☆ ☆ ☆ ☆ ☆

PLOT DEVELOPMENT

☆ ☆ ☆ ☆ ☆

QUALITY OF WRITING

☆ ☆ ☆ ☆ ☆

OVERALL

☆ ☆ ☆ ☆ ☆

TITLE: _____

AUTHOR: _____

DATE READ: _____

THOUGHTS: _____

_____

_____

_____

RATINGS

CHARACTERS

☆ ☆ ☆ ☆ ☆

PLOT DEVELOPMENT

☆ ☆ ☆ ☆ ☆

QUALITY OF WRITING

☆ ☆ ☆ ☆ ☆

OVERALL

☆ ☆ ☆ ☆ ☆

TITLE: _____

AUTHOR: _____

DATE READ: _____

THOUGHTS: _____

_____

_____

_____

RATINGS

CHARACTERS

☆ ☆ ☆ ☆ ☆

PLOT DEVELOPMENT

☆ ☆ ☆ ☆ ☆

QUALITY OF WRITING

☆ ☆ ☆ ☆ ☆

OVERALL

☆ ☆ ☆ ☆ ☆

TITLE: _____

AUTHOR: _____

DATE READ: _____

THOUGHTS: _____

_____

_____

_____

RATINGS

CHARACTERS

☆ ☆ ☆ ☆ ☆

PLOT DEVELOPMENT

☆ ☆ ☆ ☆ ☆

QUALITY OF WRITING

☆ ☆ ☆ ☆ ☆

OVERALL

☆ ☆ ☆ ☆ ☆

TITLE: _____

AUTHOR: _____

DATE READ: _____

THOUGHTS: _____

_____

_____

_____

RATINGS

CHARACTERS

☆ ☆ ☆ ☆ ☆

PLOT DEVELOPMENT

☆ ☆ ☆ ☆ ☆

QUALITY OF WRITING

☆ ☆ ☆ ☆ ☆

OVERALL

☆ ☆ ☆ ☆ ☆

TITLE: _____

AUTHOR: _____

DATE READ: _____

THOUGHTS: _____

_____

_____

_____

RATINGS

CHARACTERS

☆ ☆ ☆ ☆ ☆

PLOT DEVELOPMENT

☆ ☆ ☆ ☆ ☆

QUALITY OF WRITING

☆ ☆ ☆ ☆ ☆

OVERALL

☆ ☆ ☆ ☆ ☆

TITLE: _____

AUTHOR: _____

DATE READ: _____

THOUGHTS: _____

_____

_____

_____

RATINGS

CHARACTERS

☆ ☆ ☆ ☆ ☆

PLOT DEVELOPMENT

☆ ☆ ☆ ☆ ☆

QUALITY OF WRITING

☆ ☆ ☆ ☆ ☆

OVERALL

☆ ☆ ☆ ☆ ☆

TITLE: _____

AUTHOR: _____

DATE READ: _____

THOUGHTS: _____

_____

_____

_____

RATINGS

CHARACTERS

☆ ☆ ☆ ☆ ☆

PLOT DEVELOPMENT

☆ ☆ ☆ ☆ ☆

QUALITY OF WRITING

☆ ☆ ☆ ☆ ☆

OVERALL

☆ ☆ ☆ ☆ ☆

TITLE: _____

AUTHOR: _____

DATE READ: _____

THOUGHTS: _____

_____

_____

_____

RATINGS

CHARACTERS

☆ ☆ ☆ ☆ ☆

PLOT DEVELOPMENT

☆ ☆ ☆ ☆ ☆

QUALITY OF WRITING

☆ ☆ ☆ ☆ ☆

OVERALL

☆ ☆ ☆ ☆ ☆

> ## "'A reader lives a thousand lives before he dies,' said Jojen. 'The man who never reads lives only one.'"
>
> —GEORGE R.R. MARTIN, *A Dance with Dragons*

TITLE: _____

AUTHOR: _____

DATE READ: _____

THOUGHTS: _____

_____

_____

_____

RATINGS

CHARACTERS
☆ ☆ ☆ ☆ ☆

PLOT DEVELOPMENT
☆ ☆ ☆ ☆ ☆

QUALITY OF WRITING
☆ ☆ ☆ ☆ ☆

OVERALL
☆ ☆ ☆ ☆ ☆

TITLE: _____

AUTHOR: _____

DATE READ: _____

THOUGHTS: _____

_____

_____

_____

RATINGS

CHARACTERS
☆ ☆ ☆ ☆ ☆

PLOT DEVELOPMENT
☆ ☆ ☆ ☆ ☆

QUALITY OF WRITING
☆ ☆ ☆ ☆ ☆

OVERALL
☆ ☆ ☆ ☆ ☆

TITLE: _____

AUTHOR: _____

DATE READ: _____

THOUGHTS: _____

_____

_____

_____

RATINGS

CHARACTERS
☆ ☆ ☆ ☆ ☆

PLOT DEVELOPMENT
☆ ☆ ☆ ☆ ☆

QUALITY OF WRITING
☆ ☆ ☆ ☆ ☆

OVERALL
☆ ☆ ☆ ☆ ☆

BOOKS I'VE READ

TITLE: _____

AUTHOR: _____

DATE READ: _____

THOUGHTS: _____

_____

_____

_____

RATINGS

CHARACTERS

☆ ☆ ☆ ☆ ☆

PLOT DEVELOPMENT

☆ ☆ ☆ ☆ ☆

QUALITY OF WRITING

☆ ☆ ☆ ☆ ☆

OVERALL

☆ ☆ ☆ ☆ ☆

TITLE: _____

AUTHOR: _____

DATE READ: _____

THOUGHTS: _____

_____

_____

_____

RATINGS

CHARACTERS

☆ ☆ ☆ ☆ ☆

PLOT DEVELOPMENT

☆ ☆ ☆ ☆ ☆

QUALITY OF WRITING

☆ ☆ ☆ ☆ ☆

OVERALL

☆ ☆ ☆ ☆ ☆

TITLE: _____

AUTHOR: _____

DATE READ: _____

THOUGHTS: _____

_____

_____

_____

RATINGS

CHARACTERS

☆ ☆ ☆ ☆ ☆

PLOT DEVELOPMENT

☆ ☆ ☆ ☆ ☆

QUALITY OF WRITING

☆ ☆ ☆ ☆ ☆

OVERALL

☆ ☆ ☆ ☆ ☆

TITLE: _____

AUTHOR: _____

DATE READ: _____

THOUGHTS: _____

_____

_____

_____

RATINGS

CHARACTERS

☆ ☆ ☆ ☆ ☆

PLOT DEVELOPMENT

☆ ☆ ☆ ☆ ☆

QUALITY OF WRITING

☆ ☆ ☆ ☆ ☆

OVERALL

☆ ☆ ☆ ☆ ☆

TITLE: _____

AUTHOR: _____

DATE READ: _____

THOUGHTS: _____

_____

_____

_____

RATINGS

CHARACTERS
☆ ☆ ☆ ☆ ☆

PLOT DEVELOPMENT
☆ ☆ ☆ ☆ ☆

QUALITY OF WRITING
☆ ☆ ☆ ☆ ☆

OVERALL
☆ ☆ ☆ ☆ ☆

TITLE: _____

AUTHOR: _____

DATE READ: _____

THOUGHTS: _____

_____

_____

_____

RATINGS

CHARACTERS
☆ ☆ ☆ ☆ ☆

PLOT DEVELOPMENT
☆ ☆ ☆ ☆ ☆

QUALITY OF WRITING
☆ ☆ ☆ ☆ ☆

OVERALL
☆ ☆ ☆ ☆ ☆

TITLE: _____

AUTHOR: _____

DATE READ: _____

THOUGHTS: _____

_____

_____

_____

RATINGS

CHARACTERS
☆ ☆ ☆ ☆ ☆

PLOT DEVELOPMENT
☆ ☆ ☆ ☆ ☆

QUALITY OF WRITING
☆ ☆ ☆ ☆ ☆

OVERALL
☆ ☆ ☆ ☆ ☆

TITLE: _____

AUTHOR: _____

DATE READ: _____

THOUGHTS: _____

_____

_____

_____

RATINGS

CHARACTERS
☆ ☆ ☆ ☆ ☆

PLOT DEVELOPMENT
☆ ☆ ☆ ☆ ☆

QUALITY OF WRITING
☆ ☆ ☆ ☆ ☆

OVERALL
☆ ☆ ☆ ☆ ☆

BOOKS I'VE READ

TITLE: _____
AUTHOR: _____
DATE READ: _____
THOUGHTS: _____
_____
_____
_____

RATINGS

CHARACTERS
☆ ☆ ☆ ☆ ☆

PLOT DEVELOPMENT
☆ ☆ ☆ ☆ ☆

QUALITY OF WRITING
☆ ☆ ☆ ☆ ☆

OVERALL
☆ ☆ ☆ ☆ ☆

TITLE: _____
AUTHOR: _____
DATE READ: _____
THOUGHTS: _____
_____
_____
_____

RATINGS

CHARACTERS
☆ ☆ ☆ ☆ ☆

PLOT DEVELOPMENT
☆ ☆ ☆ ☆ ☆

QUALITY OF WRITING
☆ ☆ ☆ ☆ ☆

OVERALL
☆ ☆ ☆ ☆ ☆

"My grandfather always says that's what books are for . . . to travel without moving an inch."

—JHUMPA LAHIRI, *The Namesake*

TITLE: _____
AUTHOR: _____
DATE READ: _____
THOUGHTS: _____
_____
_____
_____

RATINGS

CHARACTERS
☆ ☆ ☆ ☆ ☆

PLOT DEVELOPMENT
☆ ☆ ☆ ☆ ☆

QUALITY OF WRITING
☆ ☆ ☆ ☆ ☆

OVERALL
☆ ☆ ☆ ☆ ☆

TITLE: _____

AUTHOR: _____

DATE READ: _____

THOUGHTS: _____

_____

_____

_____

RATINGS

CHARACTERS

☆ ☆ ☆ ☆ ☆

PLOT DEVELOPMENT

☆ ☆ ☆ ☆ ☆

QUALITY OF WRITING

☆ ☆ ☆ ☆ ☆

OVERALL

☆ ☆ ☆ ☆ ☆

TITLE: _____

AUTHOR: _____

DATE READ: _____

THOUGHTS: _____

_____

_____

_____

RATINGS

CHARACTERS

☆ ☆ ☆ ☆ ☆

PLOT DEVELOPMENT

☆ ☆ ☆ ☆ ☆

QUALITY OF WRITING

☆ ☆ ☆ ☆ ☆

OVERALL

☆ ☆ ☆ ☆ ☆

TITLE: _____

AUTHOR: _____

DATE READ: _____

THOUGHTS: _____

_____

_____

_____

RATINGS

CHARACTERS

☆ ☆ ☆ ☆ ☆

PLOT DEVELOPMENT

☆ ☆ ☆ ☆ ☆

QUALITY OF WRITING

☆ ☆ ☆ ☆ ☆

OVERALL

☆ ☆ ☆ ☆ ☆

TITLE: _____

AUTHOR: _____

DATE READ: _____

THOUGHTS: _____

_____

_____

_____

RATINGS

CHARACTERS

☆ ☆ ☆ ☆ ☆

PLOT DEVELOPMENT

☆ ☆ ☆ ☆ ☆

QUALITY OF WRITING

☆ ☆ ☆ ☆ ☆

OVERALL

☆ ☆ ☆ ☆ ☆

BOOKS I'VE READ

TITLE: _____

AUTHOR: _____

DATE READ: _____

THOUGHTS: _____

_____

_____

_____

RATINGS

CHARACTERS
☆ ☆ ☆ ☆ ☆

PLOT DEVELOPMENT
☆ ☆ ☆ ☆ ☆

QUALITY OF WRITING
☆ ☆ ☆ ☆ ☆

OVERALL
☆ ☆ ☆ ☆ ☆

TITLE: _____

AUTHOR: _____

DATE READ: _____

THOUGHTS: _____

_____

_____

_____

RATINGS

CHARACTERS
☆ ☆ ☆ ☆ ☆

PLOT DEVELOPMENT
☆ ☆ ☆ ☆ ☆

QUALITY OF WRITING
☆ ☆ ☆ ☆ ☆

OVERALL
☆ ☆ ☆ ☆ ☆

TITLE: _____

AUTHOR: _____

DATE READ: _____

THOUGHTS: _____

_____

_____

_____

RATINGS

CHARACTERS
☆ ☆ ☆ ☆ ☆

PLOT DEVELOPMENT
☆ ☆ ☆ ☆ ☆

QUALITY OF WRITING
☆ ☆ ☆ ☆ ☆

OVERALL
☆ ☆ ☆ ☆ ☆

TITLE: _____

AUTHOR: _____

DATE READ: _____

THOUGHTS: _____

_____

_____

_____

RATINGS

CHARACTERS
☆ ☆ ☆ ☆ ☆

PLOT DEVELOPMENT
☆ ☆ ☆ ☆ ☆

QUALITY OF WRITING
☆ ☆ ☆ ☆ ☆

OVERALL
☆ ☆ ☆ ☆ ☆

TITLE: _____

AUTHOR: _____

DATE READ: _____

THOUGHTS: _____

_____

_____

_____

RATINGS

CHARACTERS
☆ ☆ ☆ ☆ ☆

PLOT DEVELOPMENT
☆ ☆ ☆ ☆ ☆

QUALITY OF WRITING
☆ ☆ ☆ ☆ ☆

OVERALL
☆ ☆ ☆ ☆ ☆

"She read books as one would breathe air, to fill up and live; she read books as one would breathe ether, to sink in and die."

—ANNIE DILLARD, *The Living*

TITLE: _____

AUTHOR: _____

DATE READ: _____

THOUGHTS: _____

_____

_____

_____

RATINGS

CHARACTERS
☆ ☆ ☆ ☆ ☆

PLOT DEVELOPMENT
☆ ☆ ☆ ☆ ☆

QUALITY OF WRITING
☆ ☆ ☆ ☆ ☆

OVERALL
☆ ☆ ☆ ☆ ☆

TITLE: _____

AUTHOR: _____

DATE READ: _____

THOUGHTS: _____

_____

_____

_____

RATINGS

CHARACTERS
☆ ☆ ☆ ☆ ☆

PLOT DEVELOPMENT
☆ ☆ ☆ ☆ ☆

QUALITY OF WRITING
☆ ☆ ☆ ☆ ☆

OVERALL
☆ ☆ ☆ ☆ ☆

> **"If you only read the books that everyone else is reading, you can only think what everyone else is thinking."** —HARUKI MURAKAMI, *Norwegian Wood*

TITLE: _____

AUTHOR: _____

DATE READ: _____

THOUGHTS: _____
_____
_____
_____

RATINGS

CHARACTERS
☆ ☆ ☆ ☆ ☆

PLOT DEVELOPMENT
☆ ☆ ☆ ☆ ☆

QUALITY OF WRITING
☆ ☆ ☆ ☆ ☆

OVERALL
☆ ☆ ☆ ☆ ☆

TITLE: _____

AUTHOR: _____

DATE READ: _____

THOUGHTS: _____
_____
_____
_____

RATINGS

CHARACTERS
☆ ☆ ☆ ☆ ☆

PLOT DEVELOPMENT
☆ ☆ ☆ ☆ ☆

QUALITY OF WRITING
☆ ☆ ☆ ☆ ☆

OVERALL
☆ ☆ ☆ ☆ ☆

TITLE: _____

AUTHOR: _____

DATE READ: _____

THOUGHTS: _____
_____
_____
_____

RATINGS

CHARACTERS
☆ ☆ ☆ ☆ ☆

PLOT DEVELOPMENT
☆ ☆ ☆ ☆ ☆

QUALITY OF WRITING
☆ ☆ ☆ ☆ ☆

OVERALL
☆ ☆ ☆ ☆ ☆

TITLE: _____

AUTHOR: _____

DATE READ: _____

THOUGHTS: _____

_____

_____

_____

RATINGS

CHARACTERS

☆ ☆ ☆ ☆ ☆

PLOT DEVELOPMENT

☆ ☆ ☆ ☆ ☆

QUALITY OF WRITING

☆ ☆ ☆ ☆ ☆

OVERALL

☆ ☆ ☆ ☆ ☆

TITLE: _____

AUTHOR: _____

DATE READ: _____

THOUGHTS: _____

_____

_____

_____

RATINGS

CHARACTERS

☆ ☆ ☆ ☆ ☆

PLOT DEVELOPMENT

☆ ☆ ☆ ☆ ☆

QUALITY OF WRITING

☆ ☆ ☆ ☆ ☆

OVERALL

☆ ☆ ☆ ☆ ☆

TITLE: _____

AUTHOR: _____

DATE READ: _____

THOUGHTS: _____

_____

_____

_____

RATINGS

CHARACTERS

☆ ☆ ☆ ☆ ☆

PLOT DEVELOPMENT

☆ ☆ ☆ ☆ ☆

QUALITY OF WRITING

☆ ☆ ☆ ☆ ☆

OVERALL

☆ ☆ ☆ ☆ ☆

TITLE: _____

AUTHOR: _____

DATE READ: _____

THOUGHTS: _____

_____

_____

_____

RATINGS

CHARACTERS

☆ ☆ ☆ ☆ ☆

PLOT DEVELOPMENT

☆ ☆ ☆ ☆ ☆

QUALITY OF WRITING

☆ ☆ ☆ ☆ ☆

OVERALL

☆ ☆ ☆ ☆ ☆

BOOKS I'VE READ

TITLE: _____

AUTHOR: _____

DATE READ: _____

THOUGHTS: _____

_____

_____

_____

RATINGS

CHARACTERS
☆ ☆ ☆ ☆ ☆

PLOT DEVELOPMENT
☆ ☆ ☆ ☆ ☆

QUALITY OF WRITING
☆ ☆ ☆ ☆ ☆

OVERALL
☆ ☆ ☆ ☆ ☆

TITLE: _____

AUTHOR: _____

DATE READ: _____

THOUGHTS: _____

_____

_____

_____

RATINGS

CHARACTERS
☆ ☆ ☆ ☆ ☆

PLOT DEVELOPMENT
☆ ☆ ☆ ☆ ☆

QUALITY OF WRITING
☆ ☆ ☆ ☆ ☆

OVERALL
☆ ☆ ☆ ☆ ☆

TITLE: _____

AUTHOR: _____

DATE READ: _____

THOUGHTS: _____

_____

_____

_____

RATINGS

CHARACTERS
☆ ☆ ☆ ☆ ☆

PLOT DEVELOPMENT
☆ ☆ ☆ ☆ ☆

QUALITY OF WRITING
☆ ☆ ☆ ☆ ☆

OVERALL
☆ ☆ ☆ ☆ ☆

> **"I went away in my head, into a book. That was where I went whenever real life was too hard or too inflexible."**
>
> **—NEIL GAIMAN,** *The Ocean at the End of the Lane*

TITLE: _____

AUTHOR: _____

DATE READ: _____

THOUGHTS: _____

_____

_____

_____

RATINGS

CHARACTERS

☆ ☆ ☆ ☆ ☆

PLOT DEVELOPMENT

☆ ☆ ☆ ☆ ☆

QUALITY OF WRITING

☆ ☆ ☆ ☆ ☆

OVERALL

☆ ☆ ☆ ☆ ☆

TITLE: _____

AUTHOR: _____

DATE READ: _____

THOUGHTS: _____

_____

_____

_____

RATINGS

CHARACTERS

☆ ☆ ☆ ☆ ☆

PLOT DEVELOPMENT

☆ ☆ ☆ ☆ ☆

QUALITY OF WRITING

☆ ☆ ☆ ☆ ☆

OVERALL

☆ ☆ ☆ ☆ ☆

TITLE: _____

AUTHOR: _____

DATE READ: _____

THOUGHTS: _____

_____

_____

_____

RATINGS

CHARACTERS

☆ ☆ ☆ ☆ ☆

PLOT DEVELOPMENT

☆ ☆ ☆ ☆ ☆

QUALITY OF WRITING

☆ ☆ ☆ ☆ ☆

OVERALL

☆ ☆ ☆ ☆ ☆

TITLE: _____

AUTHOR: _____

DATE READ: _____

THOUGHTS: _____

_____

_____

_____

RATINGS

CHARACTERS

☆ ☆ ☆ ☆ ☆

PLOT DEVELOPMENT

☆ ☆ ☆ ☆ ☆

QUALITY OF WRITING

☆ ☆ ☆ ☆ ☆

OVERALL

☆ ☆ ☆ ☆ ☆

BOOKS I'VE READ

TITLE: _____

AUTHOR: _____

DATE READ: _____

THOUGHTS: _____

_____

_____

_____

RATINGS

CHARACTERS
☆ ☆ ☆ ☆ ☆

PLOT DEVELOPMENT
☆ ☆ ☆ ☆ ☆

QUALITY OF WRITING
☆ ☆ ☆ ☆ ☆

OVERALL
☆ ☆ ☆ ☆ ☆

TITLE: _____

AUTHOR: _____

DATE READ: _____

THOUGHTS: _____

_____

_____

_____

RATINGS

CHARACTERS
☆ ☆ ☆ ☆ ☆

PLOT DEVELOPMENT
☆ ☆ ☆ ☆ ☆

QUALITY OF WRITING
☆ ☆ ☆ ☆ ☆

OVERALL
☆ ☆ ☆ ☆ ☆

TITLE: _____

AUTHOR: _____

DATE READ: _____

THOUGHTS: _____

_____

_____

_____

RATINGS

CHARACTERS
☆ ☆ ☆ ☆ ☆

PLOT DEVELOPMENT
☆ ☆ ☆ ☆ ☆

QUALITY OF WRITING
☆ ☆ ☆ ☆ ☆

OVERALL
☆ ☆ ☆ ☆ ☆

TITLE: _____

AUTHOR: _____

DATE READ: _____

THOUGHTS: _____

_____

_____

_____

RATINGS

CHARACTERS
☆ ☆ ☆ ☆ ☆

PLOT DEVELOPMENT
☆ ☆ ☆ ☆ ☆

QUALITY OF WRITING
☆ ☆ ☆ ☆ ☆

OVERALL
☆ ☆ ☆ ☆ ☆

TITLE: _____

AUTHOR: _____

DATE READ: _____

THOUGHTS: _____

_____

_____

_____

_____

RATINGS

CHARACTERS
☆ ☆ ☆ ☆ ☆

PLOT DEVELOPMENT
☆ ☆ ☆ ☆ ☆

QUALITY OF WRITING
☆ ☆ ☆ ☆ ☆

OVERALL
☆ ☆ ☆ ☆ ☆

TITLE: _____

AUTHOR: _____

DATE READ: _____

THOUGHTS: _____

_____

_____

_____

_____

RATINGS

CHARACTERS
☆ ☆ ☆ ☆ ☆

PLOT DEVELOPMENT
☆ ☆ ☆ ☆ ☆

QUALITY OF WRITING
☆ ☆ ☆ ☆ ☆

OVERALL
☆ ☆ ☆ ☆ ☆

TITLE: _____

AUTHOR: _____

DATE READ: _____

THOUGHTS: _____

_____

_____

_____

_____

RATINGS

CHARACTERS
☆ ☆ ☆ ☆ ☆

PLOT DEVELOPMENT
☆ ☆ ☆ ☆ ☆

QUALITY OF WRITING
☆ ☆ ☆ ☆ ☆

OVERALL
☆ ☆ ☆ ☆ ☆

"From that time on, the world was hers for the reading. She would never be lonely again, never miss the lack of intimate friends. Books became her friends and there was one for every mood."

—BETTY SMITH, *A Tree Grows in Brooklyn*

BOOKS I'VE READ

TITLE: _____

AUTHOR: _____

DATE READ: _____

THOUGHTS: _____

_____

_____

_____

RATINGS

CHARACTERS
☆ ☆ ☆ ☆ ☆

PLOT DEVELOPMENT
☆ ☆ ☆ ☆ ☆

QUALITY OF WRITING
☆ ☆ ☆ ☆ ☆

OVERALL
☆ ☆ ☆ ☆ ☆

TITLE: _____

AUTHOR: _____

DATE READ: _____

THOUGHTS: _____

_____

_____

_____

RATINGS

CHARACTERS
☆ ☆ ☆ ☆ ☆

PLOT DEVELOPMENT
☆ ☆ ☆ ☆ ☆

QUALITY OF WRITING
☆ ☆ ☆ ☆ ☆

OVERALL
☆ ☆ ☆ ☆ ☆

TITLE: _____

AUTHOR: _____

DATE READ: _____

THOUGHTS: _____

_____

_____

_____

RATINGS

CHARACTERS
☆ ☆ ☆ ☆ ☆

PLOT DEVELOPMENT
☆ ☆ ☆ ☆ ☆

QUALITY OF WRITING
☆ ☆ ☆ ☆ ☆

OVERALL
☆ ☆ ☆ ☆ ☆

TITLE: _____

AUTHOR: _____

DATE READ: _____

THOUGHTS: _____

_____

_____

_____

RATINGS

CHARACTERS
☆ ☆ ☆ ☆ ☆

PLOT DEVELOPMENT
☆ ☆ ☆ ☆ ☆

QUALITY OF WRITING
☆ ☆ ☆ ☆ ☆

OVERALL
☆ ☆ ☆ ☆ ☆

"Books are almost as individual as friends."

—THEODORE ROOSEVELT, author of more than thirty books, in his autobiography

---

TITLE: _____

AUTHOR: _____

DATE READ: _____

THOUGHTS: _____

_____

_____

_____

RATINGS

CHARACTERS

☆ ☆ ☆ ☆ ☆

PLOT DEVELOPMENT

☆ ☆ ☆ ☆ ☆

QUALITY OF WRITING

☆ ☆ ☆ ☆ ☆

OVERALL

☆ ☆ ☆ ☆ ☆

TITLE: _____

AUTHOR: _____

DATE READ: _____

THOUGHTS: _____

_____

_____

_____

RATINGS

CHARACTERS

☆ ☆ ☆ ☆ ☆

PLOT DEVELOPMENT

☆ ☆ ☆ ☆ ☆

QUALITY OF WRITING

☆ ☆ ☆ ☆ ☆

OVERALL

☆ ☆ ☆ ☆ ☆

TITLE: _____

AUTHOR: _____

DATE READ: _____

THOUGHTS: _____

_____

_____

_____

RATINGS

CHARACTERS

☆ ☆ ☆ ☆ ☆

PLOT DEVELOPMENT

☆ ☆ ☆ ☆ ☆

QUALITY OF WRITING

☆ ☆ ☆ ☆ ☆

OVERALL

☆ ☆ ☆ ☆ ☆

"Do they sense it, these dead writers, when their books are read? Does a pinprick of light appear in their darkness? Is their soul stirred by the feather touch of another mind reading theirs? I do hope so."

—DIANE SETTERFIELD, *The Thirteenth Tale*

TITLE: _____

AUTHOR: _____

DATE READ: _____

THOUGHTS: _____

_____

_____

_____

_____

RATINGS

CHARACTERS
☆ ☆ ☆ ☆ ☆

PLOT DEVELOPMENT
☆ ☆ ☆ ☆ ☆

QUALITY OF WRITING
☆ ☆ ☆ ☆ ☆

OVERALL
☆ ☆ ☆ ☆ ☆

TITLE: _____

AUTHOR: _____

DATE READ: _____

THOUGHTS: _____

_____

_____

_____

_____

RATINGS

CHARACTERS
☆ ☆ ☆ ☆ ☆

PLOT DEVELOPMENT
☆ ☆ ☆ ☆ ☆

QUALITY OF WRITING
☆ ☆ ☆ ☆ ☆

OVERALL
☆ ☆ ☆ ☆ ☆

TITLE: _____

AUTHOR: _____

DATE READ: _____

THOUGHTS: _____

_____

_____

_____

_____

RATINGS

CHARACTERS
☆ ☆ ☆ ☆ ☆

PLOT DEVELOPMENT
☆ ☆ ☆ ☆ ☆

QUALITY OF WRITING
☆ ☆ ☆ ☆ ☆

OVERALL
☆ ☆ ☆ ☆ ☆

TITLE: _____

AUTHOR: _____

DATE READ: _____

THOUGHTS: _____

_____

_____

_____

RATINGS

CHARACTERS
☆ ☆ ☆ ☆ ☆

PLOT DEVELOPMENT
☆ ☆ ☆ ☆ ☆

QUALITY OF WRITING
☆ ☆ ☆ ☆ ☆

OVERALL
☆ ☆ ☆ ☆ ☆

TITLE: _____

AUTHOR: _____

DATE READ: _____

THOUGHTS: _____

_____

_____

_____

RATINGS

CHARACTERS
☆ ☆ ☆ ☆ ☆

PLOT DEVELOPMENT
☆ ☆ ☆ ☆ ☆

QUALITY OF WRITING
☆ ☆ ☆ ☆ ☆

OVERALL
☆ ☆ ☆ ☆ ☆

TITLE: _____

AUTHOR: _____

DATE READ: _____

THOUGHTS: _____

_____

_____

_____

RATINGS

CHARACTERS
☆ ☆ ☆ ☆ ☆

PLOT DEVELOPMENT
☆ ☆ ☆ ☆ ☆

QUALITY OF WRITING
☆ ☆ ☆ ☆ ☆

OVERALL
☆ ☆ ☆ ☆ ☆

TITLE: _____

AUTHOR: _____

DATE READ: _____

THOUGHTS: _____

_____

_____

_____

RATINGS

CHARACTERS
☆ ☆ ☆ ☆ ☆

PLOT DEVELOPMENT
☆ ☆ ☆ ☆ ☆

QUALITY OF WRITING
☆ ☆ ☆ ☆ ☆

OVERALL
☆ ☆ ☆ ☆ ☆

TITLE: _____

AUTHOR: _____

DATE READ: _____

THOUGHTS: _____

_____

_____

_____

RATINGS

CHARACTERS

☆ ☆ ☆ ☆ ☆

PLOT DEVELOPMENT

☆ ☆ ☆ ☆ ☆

QUALITY OF WRITING

☆ ☆ ☆ ☆ ☆

OVERALL

☆ ☆ ☆ ☆ ☆

TITLE: _____

AUTHOR: _____

DATE READ: _____

THOUGHTS: _____

_____

_____

_____

RATINGS

CHARACTERS

☆ ☆ ☆ ☆ ☆

PLOT DEVELOPMENT

☆ ☆ ☆ ☆ ☆

QUALITY OF WRITING

☆ ☆ ☆ ☆ ☆

OVERALL

☆ ☆ ☆ ☆ ☆

"One glance at [a book] and you hear the voice of another person—perhaps someone dead for thousands of years. Across the millennia, the author is speaking, clearly and silently, inside your head, directly to you. . . . To read is to voyage through time."
—CARL SAGAN, *Cosmos*

TITLE: _____

AUTHOR: _____

DATE READ: _____

THOUGHTS: _____

_____

_____

_____

RATINGS

CHARACTERS

☆ ☆ ☆ ☆ ☆

PLOT DEVELOPMENT

☆ ☆ ☆ ☆ ☆

QUALITY OF WRITING

☆ ☆ ☆ ☆ ☆

OVERALL

☆ ☆ ☆ ☆ ☆

I COULD WRITE FAN FICTION FOR THIS BOOK

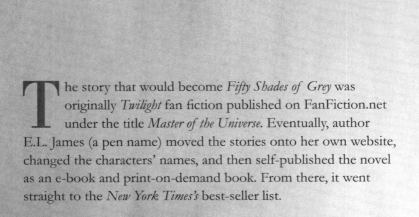

The story that would become *Fifty Shades of Grey* was originally *Twilight* fan fiction published on FanFiction.net under the title *Master of the Universe*. Eventually, author E.L. James (a pen name) moved the stories onto her own website, changed the characters' names, and then self-published the novel as an e-book and print-on-demand book. From there, it went straight to the *New York Times's* best-seller list.

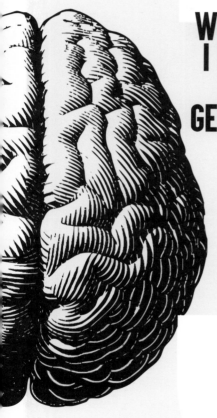

WRITERS
I THINK
ARE
GENIUSES

_____

_____

_____

3 NOVELISTS WHO WON THE MACARTHUR "GENIUS GRANT"

The MacArthur Foundation Fellowship, colloquially known as "genius grants," is today "a $625,000, no-strings-attached award to extraordinarily talented and creative individuals as an investment in their potential." Novelists who have received one include:

COLSON WHITEHEAD

Colson Whitehead was twenty-nine years old when he published his first novel, *The Intuitionist*, in 1999. It received critical acclaim, and his experimental approach to telling stories about Black American experiences would continue to earn him recognition in the years that followed. He received his MacArthur genius grant in 2002 at age thirty-two. Fourteen years later, he published his most well-known work, *The Underground Railroad*, which presents an alternate history of slavery in the South. The novel won him the 2016 National Book Award for Fiction and the 2017 Pulitzer Prize for Fiction.

THOMAS PYNCHON

Thomas Pynchon's first three novels—*V.*, *The Crying of Lot 49*, and *Gravity's Rainbow*—branded him as an exciting new voice in the postmodernist literary scene. *Gravity's Rainbow* made an especially big splash, winning him the National Book Award in 1974, which he shared with Isaac Bashevis Singer for *A Crown of Feathers and Other Stories* that year. Seventeen years passed between the publication of *Gravity's Rainbow* and the release of his next novel, *Vineland*, in 1990. During that period, he was inducted into the MacArthur Fellows class of 1988 when he was fifty-one years old.

VIET THANH NGUYEN

Literary scholar Viet Thanh Nguyen was born in Vietnam and raised in America. His remarkable debut novel, *The Sympathizer*, told from a conflicted double agent's perspective, won multiple awards, including the Pulitzer Prize for Fiction in 2016. His 2017 short story collection, *The Refugees*, explores the aftermath of the Vietnam War, including a story that mirrored his own experience.

4 RUTHLESS REJECTION LETTERS

When Louisa May Alcott wrote about her experience as a governess in the essay "How I Went Out to Service," publisher James T. Fields's stinging rejection included the line, "Stick to your teaching; you can't write." Luckily, she didn't listen to his advice—and neither did the authors who received these similarly savage rejections:

JACK KEROUAC // *On the Road*
"**Kerouac does have enormous talent of a very special kind. But this is not a well made novel, nor a saleable one nor even, I think, a good one.**

His frenetic and scrambling prose perfectly expresses the feverish travels, geographically and mentally, of the Beat Generation. But is that enough? I don't think so."

—a rejection sent to Kerouac's agent, Sterling Lord

URSULA K. LE GUIN //
The Left Hand of Darkness
"**The book is so endlessly complicated by details of reference and information ... that the very action of the story seems to be to become hopelessly bogged down, and the book, eventually, unreadable .... The whole is so dry and airless, so lacking in pace, that whatever drama and excitement the novel might have had is entirely dissipated by what does seem ... to be extraneous material.**"

—a rejection sent to Le Guin's agent

GERTRUDE STEIN // *The Making of Americans: Being a History of a Family's Progress*
"Being only one, having only one pair of eyes, having only one time, having only one life, I cannot read your M.S. three or four times. Not even one time.

Only one look, only one look is enough. Hardly one copy would sell here.

Hardly one. Hardly one."

—Arthur C. Fifield

ROBERT GALBRAITH //
The Cuckoo's Calling
"Owing to pressure of submissions, I regret we cannot reply individually or provide constructive criticism.

(A writers' group/writing course may help with the latter.)"

—a rejection from Constable & Robinson to Galbraith, a.k.a. J.K. Rowling

3 Books I Hate but Everyone Else Loves

1

TITLE: _____

AUTHOR: _____

WHY: _____

_____

_____

2

TITLE: _____

AUTHOR: _____

WHY: _____

_____

_____

3

TITLE: _____

AUTHOR: _____

WHY: _____

_____

_____

65

In Iceland, the most popular Christmas gifts aren't the latest iProducts or kitchen gadgets. They're books. Each year, Iceland celebrates what's known as *Jólabókaflóðið*: the annual Yule Book Flood, a tradition that has its roots in economic policies put in place post–World War II. At the beginning of November, each household in Iceland gets a copy of the *Bókatíðindi*, the Iceland Publishers Association's catalog of all the books that will be published that year, giving residents a chance to pick out holiday books for their friends and family. Most Icelanders unwrap a book on December 24, and afterward, they cozy up with their new volume and get reading, preferably in bed, with chocolate.

3 Books I Always Give As Gifts

TITLE: _____

AUTHOR: _____

TITLE: _____

AUTHOR: _____

TITLE: _____

AUTHOR: _____

REALLY HARSH EARLY REVIEWS OF 4 CLASSIC TWENTIETH-CENTURY NOVELS

1 *Ulysses* // **JAMES JOYCE**
Joyce's magnum opus redefined literature and was a major event upon its release in 1922. Some bought into its radical structure, but others didn't—including fellow modernist Virginia Woolf. In her diary she called *Ulysses* "an illiterate, underbred book it seems to me: the book of a self-taught working man, and we all know how distressing they are, how egotistic, insistent, raw, striking, and ultimately nauseating."

2 *Native Son* // **RICHARD WRIGHT**
Richard Wright's *Native Son*, published in 1940, is another classic American novel about the Black American experience, but the *New Statesman and Nation* found the book to be "unimpressive and silly, not even as much fun as a thriller."

3 *The Sun Also Rises* // **ERNEST HEMINGWAY**
Hemingway's debut novel about masculinity and the Lost Generation typifies the sparse and powerful writing style that his subsequent work would become known for. Some critics still believe it is his most important work. His mother, Grace, on the other hand, did not. In a letter she wrote that Hemingway kept all his life, his mother said, "What is the matter? Have you ceased to be interested in loyalty, nobility, honor and fineness in life . . . surely you have other words in your vocabulary besides 'damn' and 'bitch'— Every page fills me with a sick loathing— if I should pick up a book by any other writer with such words in it, I should read no more—but pitch it in the fire."

4 *The Naked and the Dead* // **NORMAN MAILER**
Norman Mailer's debut novel, *The Naked and the Dead*, was based on his experiences with the 112th Cavalry Regiment in the Philippines during World War II. It made many readers feel like they were actually there, but other readers, like the *New Republic*'s critic, didn't agree: "For the most part, the novel is a transcription of soldiers' talk, lusterless griping and ironed-out obscenities, too detailed and monotonous to have been imaginatively conceived for any larger purpose but too exact and literal to have been merely guessed at. . . . This doesn't mean to deny Mailer his achievement. If he has a taste for transcribing banalities, he also has a talent for it."

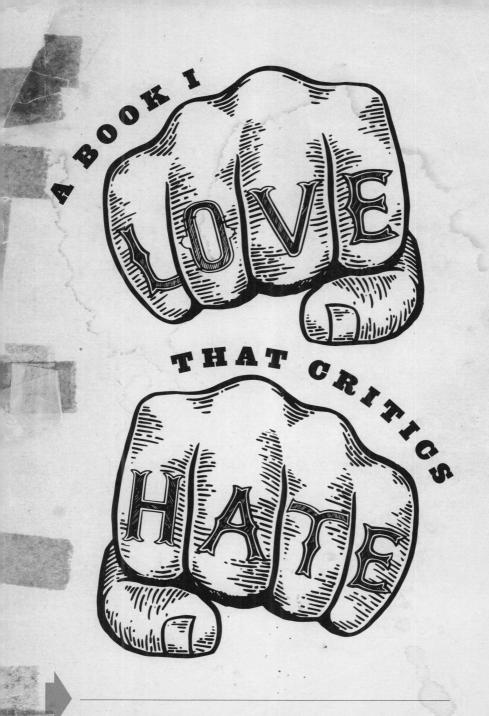

A BOOK I LOVE THAT CRITICS HATE

Books to Buy

Can't Stop Buying Books?

In English, stockpiling books without ever reading them might be called being a literary pack rat. People in Japan have a much nicer term for the habit: *tsundoku*.

According to the BBC, the term *tsundoku* derives from the words *tsumu* ("to pile up") and *doku* ("reading"), and it has been around for more than a century. One of its earliest known print appearances dates back to 1879, when a Japanese satirical text playfully referred to a professor with a large collection of unread books as *tsundoku sensei*.

BOOK SERIES TO BINGE-READ

My Struggle //
KARL OVE KNAUSGÅRD

The quotidian details of this Norwegian writer add up to so much more than the sum of their parts in this autobiographical series. You'll find yourself unable to put the books down, wondering how a seemingly inconsequential high school party from thirty years ago turned out and why you care so much.

The Millennium Series //
STIEG LARSSON

Stieg Larsson's expertly crafted psychological thrillers spawned a franchise that now includes films and additional novels written after the author passed away, but his original Millennium trilogy—*The Girl with the Dragon Tattoo*, *The Girl Who Played with Fire*, and *The Girl Who Kicked the Hornet's Nest*—is truly binge-worthy content at its finest. If you end up pulling an all-nighter (or more) to find out what wild thing Lisbeth Salander, the haunted genius at the center of the stories, does next, you won't have been the first one. To get an idea of what themes you'll encounter, Larsson's original Swedish title for *The Girl with the Dragon Tattoo* was *Men Who Hate Women*.

The Mars Trilogy //
KIM STANLEY ROBINSON

Kim Stanley Robinson's Mars trilogy imagines what humanity's inevitable presence on the Red Planet would look like, warts and all. The series begins with *Red Mars*, which details the growing pains and cultural difficulties of adjusting to life on a new planet. The next two books in the series continue to look at how humans terraform the once-dead Martian landscape into something more habitable for the long term, while escalating the drama with conflicts between rival factions vying for control.

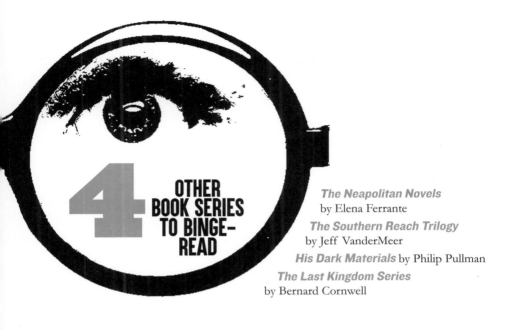

4 OTHER BOOK SERIES TO BINGE-READ

The Neapolitan Novels by Elena Ferrante
The Southern Reach Trilogy by Jeff VanderMeer
His Dark Materials by Philip Pullman
The Last Kingdom Series by Bernard Cornwell

My Favorite **BOOK SERIES**

TITLE: _____

AUTHOR: _____

WHY: _____

_____

_____

_____

_____

_____

Books on Loan

TITLE: _____
TO: _____
DATE: _____ RETURNED ☐

TITLE: _____
TO: _____
DATE: _____ RETURNED ☐

TITLE: _____
TO: _____
DATE: _____ RETURNED ☐

TITLE: _____
TO: _____
DATE: _____ RETURNED ☐

TITLE: _____
TO: _____
DATE: _____ RETURNED ☐

TITLE: _____
TO: _____
DATE: _____ RETURNED ☐

TITLE: _____
TO: _____
DATE: _____ RETURNED ☐

TITLE: _____
TO: _____
DATE: _____ RETURNED ☐

TITLE: _____
TO: _____
DATE: _____ RETURNED ☐

TITLE: _____
TO: _____
DATE: _____ RETURNED ☐

TITLE: _____
TO: _____
DATE: _____ RETURNED ☐

TITLE: _____
TO: _____
DATE: _____ RETURNED ☐

Books on Loan

TITLE: _____
TO: _____
DATE: _____ RETURNED ☐

TITLE: _____
TO: _____
DATE: _____ RETURNED ☐

TITLE: _____
TO: _____
DATE: _____ RETURNED ☐

TITLE: _____
TO: _____
DATE: _____ RETURNED ☐

TITLE: _____
TO: _____
DATE: _____ RETURNED ☐

TITLE: _____
TO: _____
DATE: _____ RETURNED ☐

TITLE: _____

TO: _____

DATE: _____ RETURNED ☐

TITLE: _____

TO: _____

DATE: _____ RETURNED ☐

TITLE: _____

TO: _____

DATE: _____ RETURNED ☐

TITLE: _____

TO: _____

DATE: _____ RETURNED ☐

TITLE: _____

TO: _____

DATE: _____ RETURNED ☐

TITLE: _____

TO: _____

DATE: _____ RETURNED ☐

Books on Loan

TITLE: _____
TO: _____
DATE: _____ RETURNED ☐

TITLE: _____
TO: _____
DATE: _____ RETURNED ☐

TITLE: _____
TO: _____
DATE: _____ RETURNED ☐

TITLE: _____
TO: _____
DATE: _____ RETURNED ☐

TITLE: _____
TO: _____
DATE: _____ RETURNED ☐

TITLE: _____
TO: _____
DATE: _____ RETURNED ☐

TITLE: _____
TO: _____
DATE: _____ RETURNED ☐

TITLE: _____
TO: _____
DATE: _____ RETURNED ☐

TITLE: _____
TO: _____
DATE: _____ RETURNED ☐

TITLE: _____
TO: _____
DATE: _____ RETURNED ☐

TITLE: _____
TO: _____
DATE: _____ RETURNED ☐

TITLE: _____
TO: _____
DATE: _____ RETURNED ☐

Books Loaned to Me

TITLE: _____
TO: _____
DATE: _____ RETURNED ☐

TITLE: _____
TO: _____
DATE: _____ RETURNED ☐

TITLE: _____
TO: _____
DATE: _____ RETURNED ☐

TITLE: _____
TO: _____
DATE: _____ RETURNED ☐

TITLE: _____
TO: _____
DATE: _____ RETURNED ☐

TITLE: _____
TO: _____
DATE: _____ RETURNED ☐

TITLE: _____
TO: _____
DATE: _____ RETURNED ☐

TITLE: _____
TO: _____
DATE: _____ RETURNED ☐

TITLE: _____
TO: _____
DATE: _____ RETURNED ☐

TITLE: _____
TO: _____
DATE: _____ RETURNED ☐

TITLE: _____
TO: _____
DATE: _____ RETURNED ☐

TITLE: _____
TO: _____
DATE: _____ RETURNED ☐

Books Loaned to Me

TITLE: _____

TO: _____

DATE: _____ RETURNED ☐

TITLE: _____

TO: _____

DATE: _____ RETURNED ☐

TITLE: _____

TO: _____

DATE: _____ RETURNED ☐

TITLE: _____

TO: _____

DATE: _____ RETURNED ☐

TITLE: _____

TO: _____

DATE: _____ RETURNED ☐

TITLE: _____

TO: _____

DATE: _____ RETURNED ☐

TITLE: _____

TO: _____

DATE: _____ RETURNED ☐

TITLE: _____

TO: _____

DATE: _____ RETURNED ☐

TITLE: _____

TO: _____

DATE: _____ RETURNED ☐

TITLE: _____

TO: _____

DATE: _____ RETURNED ☐

TITLE: _____

TO: _____

DATE: _____ RETURNED ☐

TITLE: _____

TO: _____

DATE: _____ RETURNED ☐

Books Loaned to Me

TITLE: _____
TO: _____
DATE: _____ RETURNED ☐

TITLE: _____
TO: _____
DATE: _____ RETURNED ☐

TITLE: _____
TO: _____
DATE: _____ RETURNED ☐

TITLE: _____
TO: _____
DATE: _____ RETURNED ☐

TITLE: _____
TO: _____
DATE: _____ RETURNED ☐

TITLE: _____
TO: _____
DATE: _____ RETURNED ☐

TITLE: _____

TO: _____

DATE: _____ RETURNED ☐

TITLE: _____

TO: _____

DATE: _____ RETURNED ☐

LE: _____

O: _____

E: _____ RETURNED ☐

TITLE: _____

TO: _____

DATE: _____ RETURNED ☐

TITLE: _____

TO: _____

DATE: _____ RETURNED ☐

TITLE: _____

TO: _____

DATE: _____ RETURNED ☐

NEW YORK PUBLIC LIBRARY'S
TOP 10 MOST CHECKED-OUT BOOKS

In 2020, to celebrate the 125th anniversary of the New York Public Library's 1895 opening, a team of library experts analyzed the circulation stats on all print and digital formats of books and came up with a list of the library's 10 most checked-out books of all time. The top 10 were:

1
The Snowy Day //
EZRA JACK KEATS
485,583

2
The Cat in the Hat //
DR. SEUSS
469,650

3
1984 //
GEORGE ORWELL
441,770

4
Where the Wild Things Are //
MAURICE SENDAK
436,016

5
To Kill a Mockingbird //
HARPER LEE
422,912

6
Charlotte's Web //
E.B. WHITE
337,948

7
Fahrenheit 451 //
RAY BRADBURY
316,404

8
How to Win Friends and Influence People // **DALE CARNEGIE**
284,524

9
Harry Potter and the Sorcerer's Stone // **J.K. ROWLING**
231,022

10
The Very Hungry Caterpillar //
ERIC CARLE
189,550

THE 3 LIBRARY BOOKS I'VE BORROWED MOST OFTEN

AUTHOR

AUTHOR

AUTHOR

Date Due			
JUN 2 6 '59			
JUL 1 3 '60			
___ 1 '60			
MAR 1 '60			
___ 2 8 '60			
JUL 1 2 '60			
OCT 4 '60			
NOV 4 '60			
DEC 1 '60			

4 BOOKS I ADORED AS A CHILD

_____

_____

_____

_____

Young Jack Kerouac's Reading List

I[t's no]t every day that you get a chance to peek at a reading syllabus of s[omeone] from one of the great American authors of the twentieth century. I[n 19]40, a young Jack Kerouac (then eighteen) scrawled a reading list on a [pag]e of notebook paper. The titles span eras and cultures and offer a [g]limpse at the works of literature that were molding his teenage mind. [In] two years' time, Kerouac would join the United States Merchant [Mari]ne and then the Navy, where he'd write his first attempt at a novel, [*The S]ea Is My Brother*—a work he later described as a "crock [of shit] as [litera]ture" that wouldn't be published until after his death.

[W]e all have to start somewhere.

Required Reading for J.K.

1. **Indian Scripture**
2. **Chinese [Scriptures]**
3. **Old and New Testament**
4. **Gibbon and Plutarch**
5. **Homer (again)**
6. **Shakespeare (again)**
7. **Wolfe (always)**
ETC. ETC.
"Finnegans Wake"
"Outline of History" (again)
Thoreau and Emerson ([again])
Joseph Conrad
Proust's *"Remembrance"*
Dante (again)

When *Gone Girl* author Gillian Flynn was asked about her favorite books in a 2014 Reddit AMA, she called out her "comfort food" books—the kind "you grab when you're feeling cranky and nothing sounds good to read"—which included Agatha Christie's *And Then There Were None* and Norman Mailer's *The Executioner's Song*.

MY

Comfort food

BOOKS
ARE

MY 5 FAVORITE

BESTSELLERS

ONE OF THE ALL-TIME BESTSELLERS

After Dan Brown's *The Da Vinci Code* was released in 2003, it spent a staggering 136 consecutive weeks on the *New York Times*'s best-seller list. It has sold around sixty million copies.

THE MOST
ROMANTIC
BOOK
I'VE EVER READ

TITLE:

AUTHOR:

5 GREAT LOVE STORIES IN NOVELS

Once you've read *Pride and Prejudice* and *Jane Eyre*, consider picking up these novels whose love stories will make your heart skip a beat.

1 Love in the Time of Cholera (1985) // GABRIEL GARCÍA MÁRQUEZ

Like many young loves, Florentino Ariza and Fermina Daza's secret romance is destined for heartbreak. Fermina later marries and grows old with Dr. Juvenal Urbino, a physician fighting to eradicate cholera. When her husband dies, Florentino—who continued to nurture his feelings for her, despite spending the decades engaging in many romantic affairs—attends the funeral, ready for a second chance with his first love.

2 Their Eyes Were Watching God (1937) // ZORA NEALE HURSTON

Set in early twentieth-century Florida, this Harlem Renaissance staple cemented Zora Neale Hurston's place in history as a literary great. The story, a celebration of Black love, blossoms into a complex narrative about gender roles and women's independence. Janie's love for Tea Cake is intense and imperfect, ending in tragedy, but her quest for romance and partnership rather than ownership and control celebrates a type of love that is joyful and enduring.

3 The Thorn Birds (1977) // COLLEEN MCCULLOUGH

This tale about the forbidden romance between protagonist Meggie Cleary and an older priest topped the *New York Times*'s best-seller list for more than a year. When the novel begins, Meggie is just a four-year-old child living in the harsh Australian Outback. As the decades pass, deception and death continue to dog the Cleary family. Family secrets unravel, testing both love and loyalty.

4 Norwegian Wood (1987) // HARUKI MURAKAMI

This is no lighthearted coming-of-age story. In the novel, Toru Watanabe reminisces on his years as a student in 1960s Tokyo; a time defined by love, longing, and loss. His attempts to navigate his relationships with two starkly different women, set against the backdrop of the era's civil unrest and student protests, is poignant and powerful.

5 The Notebook (1996) // NICHOLAS SPARKS

It's safe to say Sparks's entry into the literary world was a smashing one. Elderly Noah Calhoun reads a story to Allie, who is suffering from dementia. It's soon revealed that the tale he's telling is their own love story—a husband's gentle-yet-raw attempt to reignite his wife's memory of their decades-long romance.

Amy Tan's *The Joy Luck Club* wasn't written as a novel. Tan originally conceived it as a series of sixteen vignettes about four pairs of mothers and daughters, effectively making it a short story collection. But when one early review for the book referred to it as a novel, the publisher decided that was better from a marketing perspective and took "stories" off the title page. (Tan herself still considers it a collection of short stories.)

My Favorite Short Story Is

TITLE: _____

AUTHOR: _____

7 TERMS EVERY BOOK LOVER SHOULD KNOW

Bibliophiles can use these words to spice up their literary vocabulary.

Librocubicularist: A person who reads in bed. The word was coined in 1919 by Christopher Morley in *The Haunted Bookshop*.

Bibliotaph: A word, dating to the nineteeth century, that refers to a person who keeps their books "under lock and key," according to the *Oxford English Dictionary*. *Mrs. Byrne's Dictionary of Unusual, Obscure and Preposterous Words* defines it as "one who hoards or hides books." A person who steals books, meanwhile, is a biblioklept (and someone who steals and destroys books is a book-ghoul).

Book-bosomed: The *OED* defines book-bosomed as "carrying a book concealed in the bosom"—in other words, having a book on you wherever you go.

Chaptigue: Coined by Molly Schoemann-McCann on Barnes & Noble's blog in 2014, this portmanteau of "chapter" and "fatigue" is what you can use the morning after you've been up late reading.

Omnilegent: "Reading or having read everything," according to Merriam-Webster. Omnilegent dates back to 1828.

Bibliobibuli: In his 1956 book *Minority Report*, H.L. Mencken came up with this word—which combines the Greek *biblio* ("books") with the Latin *bibulus* ("drinking freely")—for "people who read too much" and are "constantly drunk on books." Sorry, H.L.: In our opinion, there's no such thing as reading too much.

Abibliophobia: Those afflicted with abibliophobia fear running out of things to read.

4 WORDS I LEARNED READING THIS YEAR

The longest book I've ever read is

Could it have been shorter?

YES   NO

When Stephen King initially submitted *The Stand* to his publisher, Doubleday, the manuscript was 1,153 pages. King was surprised to hear that the work was too long, but not for editorial reasons: The glue used in the book binding couldn't handle such a massive page count without falling apart. King ended up cutting around 150,000 words, which amounted to 400 pages, from *The Stand*. He later released an unedited version in 1990.

When Cheryl Strayed, author of the best-selling memoir *Wild*, set off on her journey up the Pacific Coast Trail, she had room to take only a few books. One was a book of Adrienne Rich's poetry, *The Dream of a Common Language*, which she had already read enough times to almost memorize it in its entirety. At one point during her arduous hike, she considered burning the book to save weight in her pack, as she had done with other books she read along the trail. "There was no reason not to burn this book too," she wrote. "Instead, I only hugged it to my chest."

3 Books I'd Take to a Desert Island

TITLE: _____

WHY: _____

_____

TITLE: _____

WHY: _____

_____

TITLE: _____

WHY: _____

_____

Bookstores Owned by FAMOUS AUTHORS

PARNASSUS BOOKS // Nashville, Tennessee:
Co-owned by *Bel Canto* author, Ann Patchett

AN UNLIKELY STORY // Plainville, Massachusetts:
Co-owned by Jeff Kinney, author of *Diary of a Wimpy Kid*

BIRCHBARK BOOKS & NATIVE ARTS // Minneapolis, Minnesota:
Owned by *The Round House* author, Louise Erdrich

BEASTLY BOOKS // Santa Fe, New Mexico:
Owned by George R.R. Martin, author of *A Game of Thrones*

BOOKS ARE MAGIC // Brooklyn, New York:
Co-owned by *Modern Lovers* author, Emma Straub

3 BOOKSTORES I WANT TO VISIT

1
NAME: _____
LOCATION: _____

2
NAME: _____
LOCATION: _____

3
NAME: _____
LOCATION: _____

TITLE: _____
AUTHOR: _____
RECOMMENDED BY: _____
WHY: _____
_____
_____
_____

DID IT! ☐

CHARACTERS
☆ ☆ ☆ ☆ ☆

PLOT DEVELOPMENT
☆ ☆ ☆ ☆ ☆

QUALITY OF WRITING
☆ ☆ ☆ ☆ ☆

OVERALL
☆ ☆ ☆ ☆ ☆

TITLE: _____
AUTHOR: _____
RECOMMENDED BY: _____
WHY: _____
_____
_____
_____

DID IT! ☐

CHARACTERS
☆ ☆ ☆ ☆ ☆

PLOT DEVELOPMENT
☆ ☆ ☆ ☆ ☆

QUALITY OF WRITING
☆ ☆ ☆ ☆ ☆

OVERALL
☆ ☆ ☆ ☆ ☆

TITLE: _____
AUTHOR: _____
RECOMMENDED BY: _____
WHY: _____
_____
_____
_____

DID IT! ☐

CHARACTERS
☆ ☆ ☆ ☆ ☆

PLOT DEVELOPMENT
☆ ☆ ☆ ☆ ☆

QUALITY OF WRITING
☆ ☆ ☆ ☆ ☆

OVERALL
☆ ☆ ☆ ☆ ☆

TITLE: _____
AUTHOR: _____
RECOMMENDED BY: _____
WHY: _____
_____
_____
_____

DID IT! ☐

CHARACTERS
☆ ☆ ☆ ☆ ☆

PLOT DEVELOPMENT
☆ ☆ ☆ ☆ ☆

QUALITY OF WRITING
☆ ☆ ☆ ☆ ☆

OVERALL
☆ ☆ ☆ ☆ ☆

BOOKS I WANT TO READ

TITLE: _____
AUTHOR: _____
RECOMMENDED BY: _____
WHY: _____
_____
_____
_____

DID IT! ☐
CHARACTERS
☆ ☆ ☆ ☆ ☆
PLOT DEVELOPMENT
☆ ☆ ☆ ☆ ☆
QUALITY OF WRITING
☆ ☆ ☆ ☆ ☆
OVERALL
☆ ☆ ☆ ☆ ☆

TITLE: _____
AUTHOR: _____
RECOMMENDED BY: _____
WHY: _____
_____
_____
_____

DID IT! ☐
CHARACTERS
☆ ☆ ☆ ☆ ☆
PLOT DEVELOPMENT
☆ ☆ ☆ ☆ ☆
QUALITY OF WRITING
☆ ☆ ☆ ☆ ☆
OVERALL
☆ ☆ ☆ ☆ ☆

TITLE: _____
AUTHOR: _____
RECOMMENDED BY: _____
WHY: _____
_____
_____
_____

DID IT! ☐
CHARACTERS
☆ ☆ ☆ ☆ ☆
PLOT DEVELOPMENT
☆ ☆ ☆ ☆ ☆
QUALITY OF WRITING
☆ ☆ ☆ ☆ ☆
OVERALL
☆ ☆ ☆ ☆ ☆

TITLE: _____
AUTHOR: _____
RECOMMENDED BY: _____
WHY: _____
_____
_____
_____

DID IT! ☐
CHARACTERS
☆ ☆ ☆ ☆ ☆
PLOT DEVELOPMENT
☆ ☆ ☆ ☆ ☆
QUALITY OF WRITING
☆ ☆ ☆ ☆ ☆
OVERALL
☆ ☆ ☆ ☆ ☆

> ## "Until I feared I would lose it, I never loved to read. One does not love breathing."
>
> —HARPER LEE, *To Kill a Mockingbird*

TITLE: _____

AUTHOR: _____

RECOMMENDED BY: _____

WHY: _____

_____

_____

_____

DID IT! ☐

CHARACTERS
☆ ☆ ☆ ☆ ☆

PLOT DEVELOPMENT
☆ ☆ ☆ ☆ ☆

QUALITY OF WRITING
☆ ☆ ☆ ☆ ☆

OVERALL
☆ ☆ ☆ ☆ ☆

TITLE: _____

AUTHOR: _____

RECOMMENDED BY: _____

WHY: _____

_____

_____

_____

DID IT! ☐

CHARACTERS
☆ ☆ ☆ ☆ ☆

PLOT DEVELOPMENT
☆ ☆ ☆ ☆ ☆

QUALITY OF WRITING
☆ ☆ ☆ ☆ ☆

OVERALL
☆ ☆ ☆ ☆ ☆

TITLE: _____

AUTHOR: _____

RECOMMENDED BY: _____

WHY: _____

_____

_____

_____

DID IT! ☐

CHARACTERS
☆ ☆ ☆ ☆ ☆

PLOT DEVELOPMENT
☆ ☆ ☆ ☆ ☆

QUALITY OF WRITING
☆ ☆ ☆ ☆ ☆

OVERALL
☆ ☆ ☆ ☆ ☆

TITLE: _____

AUTHOR: _____

RECOMMENDED BY: _____

WHY: _____

_____

_____

_____

DID IT! ☐

CHARACTERS
☆ ☆ ☆ ☆ ☆

PLOT DEVELOPMENT
☆ ☆ ☆ ☆ ☆

QUALITY OF WRITING
☆ ☆ ☆ ☆ ☆

OVERALL
☆ ☆ ☆ ☆ ☆

TITLE: _____

AUTHOR: _____

RECOMMENDED BY: _____

WHY: _____

_____

_____

_____

DID IT! ☐

CHARACTERS
☆ ☆ ☆ ☆ ☆

PLOT DEVELOPMENT
☆ ☆ ☆ ☆ ☆

QUALITY OF WRITING
☆ ☆ ☆ ☆ ☆

OVERALL
☆ ☆ ☆ ☆ ☆

> "Some books are to be tasted, others to be swallowed, and some few to be chewed and digested; that is, some books are to be read only in parts; others to be read, but not curiously; and some few to be read wholly, and with diligence and attention."
>
> —FRANCIS BACON, *Essays*

TITLE: _____

AUTHOR: _____

RECOMMENDED BY: _____

WHY: _____

_____

_____

_____

DID IT! ☐

CHARACTERS
☆ ☆ ☆ ☆ ☆

PLOT DEVELOPMENT
☆ ☆ ☆ ☆ ☆

QUALITY OF WRITING
☆ ☆ ☆ ☆ ☆

OVERALL
☆ ☆ ☆ ☆ ☆

TITLE: _____

AUTHOR: _____

RECOMMENDED BY: _____

WHY: _____

_____

_____

_____

DID IT! ☐

CHARACTERS
☆ ☆ ☆ ☆ ☆

PLOT DEVELOPMENT
☆ ☆ ☆ ☆ ☆

QUALITY OF WRITING
☆ ☆ ☆ ☆ ☆

OVERALL
☆ ☆ ☆ ☆ ☆

TITLE: _____

AUTHOR: _____

RECOMMENDED BY: _____

WHY: _____

_____

_____

_____

DID IT! ☐

CHARACTERS
☆ ☆ ☆ ☆ ☆

PLOT DEVELOPMENT
☆ ☆ ☆ ☆ ☆

QUALITY OF WRITING
☆ ☆ ☆ ☆ ☆

OVERALL
☆ ☆ ☆ ☆ ☆

TITLE: _____

AUTHOR: _____

RECOMMENDED BY: _____

WHY: _____

_____

_____

_____

DID IT! ☐

CHARACTERS
☆ ☆ ☆ ☆ ☆

PLOT DEVELOPMENT
☆ ☆ ☆ ☆ ☆

QUALITY OF WRITING
☆ ☆ ☆ ☆ ☆

OVERALL
☆ ☆ ☆ ☆ ☆

BOOKS I WANT TO READ

TITLE: _____

AUTHOR: _____

RECOMMENDED BY: _____

WHY: _____

_____

_____

_____

DID IT! ☐

CHARACTERS
☆ ☆ ☆ ☆ ☆

PLOT DEVELOPMENT
☆ ☆ ☆ ☆ ☆

QUALITY OF WRITING
☆ ☆ ☆ ☆ ☆

OVERALL
☆ ☆ ☆ ☆ ☆

TITLE: _____

AUTHOR: _____

RECOMMENDED BY: _____

WHY: _____

_____

_____

_____

DID IT! ☐

CHARACTERS
☆ ☆ ☆ ☆ ☆

PLOT DEVELOPMENT
☆ ☆ ☆ ☆ ☆

QUALITY OF WRITING
☆ ☆ ☆ ☆ ☆

OVERALL
☆ ☆ ☆ ☆ ☆

TITLE: _____

AUTHOR: _____

RECOMMENDED BY: _____

WHY: _____

_____

_____

_____

DID IT! ☐

CHARACTERS
☆ ☆ ☆ ☆ ☆

PLOT DEVELOPMENT
☆ ☆ ☆ ☆ ☆

QUALITY OF WRITING
☆ ☆ ☆ ☆ ☆

OVERALL
☆ ☆ ☆ ☆ ☆

TITLE: _____

AUTHOR: _____

RECOMMENDED BY: _____

WHY: _____

_____

_____

_____

DID IT! ☐

CHARACTERS
☆ ☆ ☆ ☆ ☆

PLOT DEVELOPMENT
☆ ☆ ☆ ☆ ☆

QUALITY OF WRITING
☆ ☆ ☆ ☆ ☆

OVERALL
☆ ☆ ☆ ☆ ☆

TITLE: _____

AUTHOR: _____

RECOMMENDED BY: _____

WHY: _____

_____

_____

_____

DID IT! ☐

CHARACTERS
☆ ☆ ☆ ☆ ☆

PLOT DEVELOPMENT
☆ ☆ ☆ ☆ ☆

QUALITY OF WRITING
☆ ☆ ☆ ☆ ☆

OVERALL
☆ ☆ ☆ ☆ ☆

TITLE: _____

AUTHOR: _____

RECOMMENDED BY: _____

WHY: _____

_____

_____

_____

DID IT! ☐

CHARACTERS
☆ ☆ ☆ ☆ ☆

PLOT DEVELOPMENT
☆ ☆ ☆ ☆ ☆

QUALITY OF WRITING
☆ ☆ ☆ ☆ ☆

OVERALL
☆ ☆ ☆ ☆ ☆

"Travel far, pay no fare, let a story take you there!"
—ANNE LINDBERGH, _Travel Far, Pay No Fare_

TITLE: _____

AUTHOR: _____

RECOMMENDED BY: _____

WHY: _____

_____

_____

_____

DID IT! ☐

CHARACTERS
☆ ☆ ☆ ☆ ☆

PLOT DEVELOPMENT
☆ ☆ ☆ ☆ ☆

QUALITY OF WRITING
☆ ☆ ☆ ☆ ☆

OVERALL
☆ ☆ ☆ ☆ ☆

TITLE: _____

AUTHOR: _____

RECOMMENDED BY: _____

WHY: _____

_____

_____

_____

DID IT! ☐

CHARACTERS
☆ ☆ ☆ ☆ ☆

PLOT DEVELOPMENT
☆ ☆ ☆ ☆ ☆

QUALITY OF WRITING
☆ ☆ ☆ ☆ ☆

OVERALL
☆ ☆ ☆ ☆ ☆

TITLE: _____

AUTHOR: _____

RECOMMENDED BY: _____

WHY: _____

_____

_____

_____

DID IT! ☐

CHARACTERS
☆ ☆ ☆ ☆ ☆

PLOT DEVELOPMENT
☆ ☆ ☆ ☆ ☆

QUALITY OF WRITING
☆ ☆ ☆ ☆ ☆

OVERALL
☆ ☆ ☆ ☆ ☆

> "Bread and books: food for the body and food for the soul—what could be more worthy of our respect, and even love?"
>
> —SALMAN RUSHDIE, *Imaginary Homelands*

TITLE: _____

AUTHOR: _____

RECOMMENDED BY: _____

WHY: _____

_____

_____

_____

DID IT! ☐

CHARACTERS
☆ ☆ ☆ ☆ ☆

PLOT DEVELOPMENT
☆ ☆ ☆ ☆ ☆

QUALITY OF WRITING
☆ ☆ ☆ ☆ ☆

OVERALL
☆ ☆ ☆ ☆ ☆

TITLE: _____

AUTHOR: _____

RECOMMENDED BY: _____

WHY: _____

_____

_____

_____

DID IT! ☐

CHARACTERS
☆ ☆ ☆ ☆ ☆

PLOT DEVELOPMENT
☆ ☆ ☆ ☆ ☆

QUALITY OF WRITING
☆ ☆ ☆ ☆ ☆

OVERALL
☆ ☆ ☆ ☆ ☆

TITLE: _____

AUTHOR: _____

RECOMMENDED BY: _____

WHY: _____

_____

_____

_____

DID IT! ☐

CHARACTERS
☆ ☆ ☆ ☆ ☆

PLOT DEVELOPMENT
☆ ☆ ☆ ☆ ☆

QUALITY OF WRITING
☆ ☆ ☆ ☆ ☆

OVERALL
☆ ☆ ☆ ☆ ☆

TITLE: _____

AUTHOR: _____

RECOMMENDED BY: _____

WHY: _____

_____

_____

_____

DID IT! ☐

CHARACTERS
☆ ☆ ☆ ☆ ☆

PLOT DEVELOPMENT
☆ ☆ ☆ ☆ ☆

QUALITY OF WRITING
☆ ☆ ☆ ☆ ☆

OVERALL
☆ ☆ ☆ ☆ ☆

TITLE: _____

AUTHOR: _____

RECOMMENDED BY: _____

WHY: _____

_____

_____

_____

DID IT! ☐

CHARACTERS
☆ ☆ ☆ ☆ ☆

PLOT DEVELOPMENT
☆ ☆ ☆ ☆ ☆

QUALITY OF WRITING
☆ ☆ ☆ ☆ ☆

OVERALL
☆ ☆ ☆ ☆ ☆

BOOKS I WANT TO READ

TITLE: _____
AUTHOR: _____
RECOMMENDED BY: _____
WHY: _____
_____
_____
_____

DID IT! ☐
CHARACTERS
☆ ☆ ☆ ☆ ☆
PLOT DEVELOPMENT
☆ ☆ ☆ ☆ ☆
QUALITY OF WRITING
☆ ☆ ☆ ☆ ☆
OVERALL
☆ ☆ ☆ ☆ ☆

TITLE: _____
AUTHOR: _____
RECOMMENDED BY: _____
WHY: _____
_____
_____
_____

DID IT! ☐
CHARACTERS
☆ ☆ ☆ ☆ ☆
PLOT DEVELOPMENT
☆ ☆ ☆ ☆ ☆
QUALITY OF WRITING
☆ ☆ ☆ ☆ ☆
OVERALL
☆ ☆ ☆ ☆ ☆

TITLE: _____
AUTHOR: _____
RECOMMENDED BY: _____
WHY: _____
_____
_____
_____

DID IT! ☐
CHARACTERS
☆ ☆ ☆ ☆ ☆
PLOT DEVELOPMENT
☆ ☆ ☆ ☆ ☆
QUALITY OF WRITING
☆ ☆ ☆ ☆ ☆
OVERALL
☆ ☆ ☆ ☆ ☆

TITLE: _____
AUTHOR: _____
RECOMMENDED BY: _____
WHY: _____
_____
_____
_____

DID IT! ☐
CHARACTERS
☆ ☆ ☆ ☆ ☆
PLOT DEVELOPMENT
☆ ☆ ☆ ☆ ☆
QUALITY OF WRITING
☆ ☆ ☆ ☆ ☆
OVERALL
☆ ☆ ☆ ☆ ☆

> # "The America I loved still exists at the front desks of our public libraries."
>
> —KURT VONNEGUT, "A Man Without a Country"

TITLE: _____

AUTHOR: _____

RECOMMENDED BY: _____

WHY: _____

_____

_____

_____

DID IT! ☐

CHARACTERS
☆ ☆ ☆ ☆ ☆

PLOT DEVELOPMENT
☆ ☆ ☆ ☆ ☆

QUALITY OF WRITING
☆ ☆ ☆ ☆ ☆

OVERALL
☆ ☆ ☆ ☆ ☆

TITLE: _____

AUTHOR: _____

RECOMMENDED BY: _____

WHY: _____

_____

_____

_____

DID IT! ☐

CHARACTERS
☆ ☆ ☆ ☆ ☆

PLOT DEVELOPMENT
☆ ☆ ☆ ☆ ☆

QUALITY OF WRITING
☆ ☆ ☆ ☆ ☆

OVERALL
☆ ☆ ☆ ☆ ☆

TITLE: _____

AUTHOR: _____

RECOMMENDED BY: _____

WHY: _____

_____

_____

_____

DID IT! ☐

CHARACTERS
☆ ☆ ☆ ☆ ☆

PLOT DEVELOPMENT
☆ ☆ ☆ ☆ ☆

QUALITY OF WRITING
☆ ☆ ☆ ☆ ☆

OVERALL
☆ ☆ ☆ ☆ ☆

TITLE: _____

AUTHOR: _____

RECOMMENDED BY: _____

WHY: _____

_____

_____

_____

DID IT! ☐

CHARACTERS

☆ ☆ ☆ ☆ ☆

PLOT DEVELOPMENT

☆ ☆ ☆ ☆ ☆

QUALITY OF WRITING

☆ ☆ ☆ ☆ ☆

OVERALL

☆ ☆ ☆ ☆ ☆

TITLE: _____

AUTHOR: _____

RECOMMENDED BY: _____

WHY: _____

_____

_____

_____

DID IT! ☐

CHARACTERS

☆ ☆ ☆ ☆ ☆

PLOT DEVELOPMENT

☆ ☆ ☆ ☆ ☆

QUALITY OF WRITING

☆ ☆ ☆ ☆ ☆

OVERALL

☆ ☆ ☆ ☆ ☆

TITLE: _____

AUTHOR: _____

RECOMMENDED BY: _____

WHY: _____

_____

_____

_____

DID IT! ☐

CHARACTERS

☆ ☆ ☆ ☆ ☆

PLOT DEVELOPMENT

☆ ☆ ☆ ☆ ☆

QUALITY OF WRITING

☆ ☆ ☆ ☆ ☆

OVERALL

☆ ☆ ☆ ☆ ☆

TITLE: _____

AUTHOR: _____

RECOMMENDED BY: _____

WHY: _____

_____

_____

_____

DID IT! ☐

CHARACTERS

☆ ☆ ☆ ☆ ☆

PLOT DEVELOPMENT

☆ ☆ ☆ ☆ ☆

QUALITY OF WRITING

☆ ☆ ☆ ☆ ☆

OVERALL

☆ ☆ ☆ ☆ ☆

TITLE: _____

AUTHOR: _____

RECOMMENDED BY: _____

WHY: _____

_____

_____

DID IT! ☐

CHARACTERS
☆ ☆ ☆ ☆ ☆

PLOT DEVELOPMENT
☆ ☆ ☆ ☆ ☆

QUALITY OF WRITING
☆ ☆ ☆ ☆ ☆

OVERALL
☆ ☆ ☆ ☆ ☆

TITLE: _____

AUTHOR: _____

RECOMMENDED BY: _____

WHY: _____

_____

_____

DID IT! ☐

CHARACTERS
☆ ☆ ☆ ☆ ☆

PLOT DEVELOPMENT
☆ ☆ ☆ ☆ ☆

QUALITY OF WRITING
☆ ☆ ☆ ☆ ☆

OVERALL
☆ ☆ ☆ ☆ ☆

TITLE: _____

AUTHOR: _____

RECOMMENDED BY: _____

WHY: _____

_____

_____

DID IT! ☐

CHARACTERS
☆ ☆ ☆ ☆ ☆

PLOT DEVELOPMENT
☆ ☆ ☆ ☆ ☆

QUALITY OF WRITING
☆ ☆ ☆ ☆ ☆

OVERALL
☆ ☆ ☆ ☆ ☆

> "I would be most content if my children grew up to be the kind of people who think decorating consists mostly of building enough bookshelves."
>
> —ANNA QUINDLEN, *The New York Times*

TITLE: _____

AUTHOR: _____

RECOMMENDED BY: _____

WHY: _____

_____

_____

_____

DID IT! ☐

CHARACTERS
☆ ☆ ☆ ☆ ☆

PLOT DEVELOPMENT
☆ ☆ ☆ ☆ ☆

QUALITY OF WRITING
☆ ☆ ☆ ☆ ☆

OVERALL
☆ ☆ ☆ ☆ ☆

TITLE: _____

AUTHOR: _____

RECOMMENDED BY: _____

WHY: _____

_____

_____

_____

DID IT! ☐

CHARACTERS
☆ ☆ ☆ ☆ ☆

PLOT DEVELOPMENT
☆ ☆ ☆ ☆ ☆

QUALITY OF WRITING
☆ ☆ ☆ ☆ ☆

OVERALL
☆ ☆ ☆ ☆ ☆

> **"[Reading] is the sole means by which we slip, involuntarily, often helplessly, into another's skin; another's voice; another's soul."**
> —JOYCE CAROL OATES, "Literature As Pleasure, Pleasure As Literature"

TITLE: _____

AUTHOR: _____

RECOMMENDED BY: _____

WHY: _____

_____

_____

_____

DID IT! ☐

CHARACTERS
☆ ☆ ☆ ☆ ☆

PLOT DEVELOPMENT
☆ ☆ ☆ ☆ ☆

QUALITY OF WRITING
☆ ☆ ☆ ☆ ☆

OVERALL
☆ ☆ ☆ ☆ ☆

TITLE: _____

AUTHOR: _____

RECOMMENDED BY: _____

WHY: _____

_____

_____

_____

DID IT! ☐

CHARACTERS

☆ ☆ ☆ ☆ ☆

PLOT DEVELOPMENT

☆ ☆ ☆ ☆ ☆

QUALITY OF WRITING

☆ ☆ ☆ ☆ ☆

OVERALL

☆ ☆ ☆ ☆ ☆

TITLE: _____

AUTHOR: _____

RECOMMENDED BY: _____

WHY: _____

_____

_____

_____

DID IT! ☐

CHARACTERS

☆ ☆ ☆ ☆ ☆

PLOT DEVELOPMENT

☆ ☆ ☆ ☆ ☆

QUALITY OF WRITING

☆ ☆ ☆ ☆ ☆

OVERALL

☆ ☆ ☆ ☆ ☆

TITLE: _____

AUTHOR: _____

RECOMMENDED BY: _____

WHY: _____

_____

_____

_____

DID IT! ☐

CHARACTERS

☆ ☆ ☆ ☆ ☆

PLOT DEVELOPMENT

☆ ☆ ☆ ☆ ☆

QUALITY OF WRITING

☆ ☆ ☆ ☆ ☆

OVERALL

☆ ☆ ☆ ☆ ☆

TITLE: _____

AUTHOR: _____

RECOMMENDED BY: _____

WHY: _____

_____

_____

_____

DID IT! ☐

CHARACTERS

☆ ☆ ☆ ☆ ☆

PLOT DEVELOPMENT

☆ ☆ ☆ ☆ ☆

QUALITY OF WRITING

☆ ☆ ☆ ☆ ☆

OVERALL

☆ ☆ ☆ ☆ ☆

5 FAMOUS NOVELISTS' HOMES YOU CAN VISIT

Who wouldn't want to see, with their own eyes, the places where great novelists did their work? Many homes of famous novelists have opened their doors to the public—here are just a few that you can put on your vacation itinerary:

Thomas Hardy's Max Gate
LOCATION: **DORCHESTER, DORSET, ENGLAND**

Hardy was both an author and an architect, and he designed Max (named after a local tollkeeper whose name was not Max but Mack) House in 1885. He wrote *Tess of the d'Urbervilles* and *Jude the Obscure* in the Victorian-style home, whose gardens are still as they were originally planned. You can also visit the cob-and-thatch cottage where Hardy was born, located just outside Dorchester.

Leo Tolstoy's Yasnaya Polyana
LOCATION: **TULA, RUSSIA**

Tolstoy was born at this Central Russian estate, which had belonged to his family since the 1760s. The writer himself inherited the estate in 1847, and wrote many of his classic works there, including *War and Peace*. Today, Yasnaya Polyana has the estate's original furniture and library and looks just as it did in the late eighteenth and early nineteenth centuries.

Pearl S. Buck's Houses
LOCATIONS: **CHINA; WEST VIRGINIA; PENNSYLVANIA**

Those heading to China can put two Pearl S. Buck homes on their itinerary: the two-story Dengyun Hill house in Zhenjiang City, where she lived for a time, and the Pearl S. Buck Memorial House on the grounds of Nanjing University, where she wrote *The Good Earth*. Those planning a trip stateside also have two potential places to visit: Her West Virginia birthplace and the Pearl S. Buck House near Dublin, Pennsylvania, where Buck moved after returning from China. She and her second husband raised their large family of adopted children there, and visitors can see everything from their closet full of board games and the typewriter Buck used to write her most famous work to the property's cultural center and the author's grave.

Johann Wolfgang von Goethe's House
LOCATION: **FRANKFURT, GERMANY**

Before he kicked off the Romantic movement, Johann Wolfgang von Goethe was just a kid growing up with sister Cornelia in a four-story bourgeois-style house in Frankfurt. Today, Goethe's birthplace has been turned into a museum

LITERARY PLACES I'D LIKE TO VISIT

where visitors can see where Goethe was supposedly born as well as the room where he wrote his early works, including *The Sorrows of Young Werther*. There's also a grand staircase that takes up a third of the building, a puppet theater room, and lavishly decorated rooms for entertaining.

La Maison de Colette
LOCATION: **SAINT-SAUVEUR EN PUISAYE, FRANCE**

Sidonie-Gabrielle Colette, a.k.a. Colette, was born at this home in 1873, and lived there until the age of eighteen, when financial issues forced her family to sell. The house and its grounds frequently pop up in the author's books, including *Claudine at School*, *The Vagabond*, and *Gigi*. Today, the home has been renovated and restored with the late nineteenth-century décor "of Colette's happy childhood," in the words of the museum's director. There are no barriers or displays; instead, the house is meant to be less like a museum and more like a home, where Colette herself could walk in at any moment.

My favorite self-published book is

James Redfield's *The Celestine Prophecy* began with a three-thousand-copy print run that set the author back about $7,000. Redfield and his wife packed up their van and spent a month at a time traveling to independent bookstores across the nation to give a copy to each manager and whatever customers were present, reprinting as needed. The strategy reinforced the old publishing adage that the best way to sell books is by word of mouth: After a few months on the road, Redfield said that everybody was talking about it, and he estimates that they had sold around 160,000 copies.

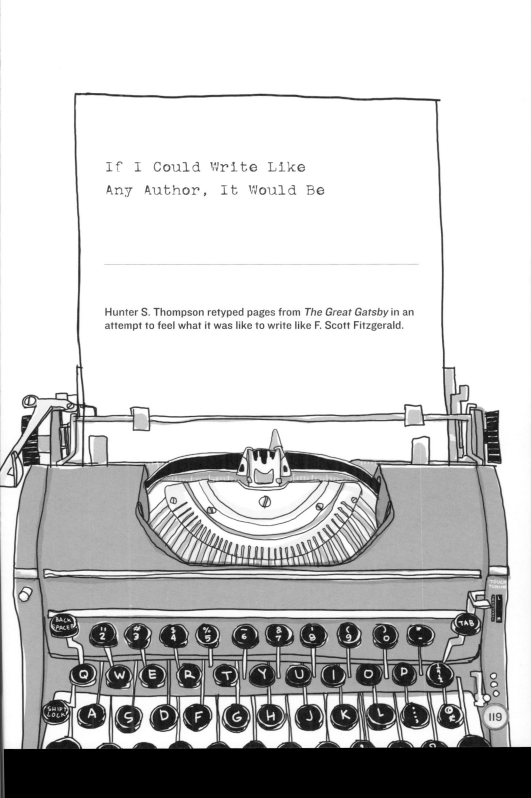

If I Could Write Like
Any Author, It Would Be

Hunter S. Thompson retyped pages from *The Great Gatsby* in an attempt to feel what it was like to write like F. Scott Fitzgerald.

The Best Movie Adaptations of Books

TITLE: _____

WHY: _____

_____

TITLE: _____

WHY: _____

_____

TITLE: _____

WHY: _____

_____

TITLE: _____

WHY: _____

_____

TITLE: _____

WHY: _____

_____

TITLE: _____

WHY: _____

_____

TITLE: _____

WHY: _____

_____

TITLE: _____

WHY: _____

AUTHORS WHO HATED MOVIE VERSIONS OF THEIR WRITING

1 WINSTON GROOM //
Forrest Gump

Note to filmmakers: Don't anger the author of the book before its sequel has been written. On the first page of the sequel, author Winston Groom wrote, "Don't never let nobody make a movie of your life's story," and "Whether they get it right or wrong, it don't matter." You can't blame Groom for being mad: He was promised 3 percent net profits from the film, which he hadn't received because producers claimed that by the time they took out production costs and advertising and promotional costs, the movie didn't turn a profit. To add insult to injury, Groom wasn't mentioned in any of the six Academy Award acceptance speeches given by various cast and crew members of *Forrest Gump*.

2 ANTHONY BURGESS //
A Clockwork Orange

Not only did Anthony Burgess dislike the movie based on his novella *A Clockwork Orange*, he later regretted writing any of it in the first place. "The book I am best known for, or only known for, is a novel I am prepared to repudiate: written a quarter of a century ago, a *jeu d'esprit* knocked off for money in three weeks, it became known as the raw material for a film which seemed to glorify sex and violence. The film made it easy for readers of the book to misunderstand what it was about, and the misunderstanding will pursue me till I die. I should not have written the book because of this danger of misinterpretation."

3 BRET EASTON ELLIS //
American Psycho

Bret Easton Ellis doesn't think any of the film adaptations of his books are that great (save for maybe *The Rules of Attraction*), but he dislikes some more than others. The author believes *American Psycho* never should have happened: "*American Psycho* was a book I didn't think needed to be turned into a movie. I think the problem with *American Psycho* was that it was conceived as a novel, as a literary work with a very unreliable narrator at the center of it and the medium of film demands answers. It demands answers. You can be as ambiguous as you want with a movie, but it doesn't matter—we're still looking at it. It's still being answered for us visually. I don't think *American Psycho* is particularly more interesting if you knew that he did it or think that it all happens in his head. I think the answer to that question makes the book infinitely less interesting."

4 KEN KESEY // One Flew Over The Cuckoo's Nest

Despite the fact that *One Flew Over the Cuckoo's Nest* swept the Academy Awards—it won Best Picture, Best Director, Best Actor, Best Actress, and Best Adapted Screenplay—author Ken Kesey was not impressed. He was originally slated to help with the production, but left not long into the process. He claimed for a long time that he didn't even watch it and was especially upset that they didn't keep the viewpoint of Chief Bromden.

MY FAVORITE SUMMER READS

TITLE: _____

AUTHOR: _____

TITLE: _____

AUTHOR: _____

TITLE: _____

AUTHOR: _____

TITLE: _____

AUTHOR: _____

TITLE: _____

AUTHOR: _____

TITLE: _____

AUTHOR: _____

Looking for a Summer Read?

For inspiration, here are a few recent novels that were #1 on the *New York Times* Hardcover Fiction Bestseller list on the summer solstice:

The Vanishing Half by **BRIT BENNETT** (2020)

Where the Crawdads Sing by **DELIA OWENS** (2019)

The Outsider by **STEPHEN KING** (2018)

Come Sundown by **NORA ROBERTS** (2017)

The Emperor's Revenge by **CLIVE CUSSLER** and **BOYD MORRISON** (2016)

FAMOUS AUTHORS' UNFINISHED MANUSCRIPTS

What do we do when an author dies with their work unfinished? Do we let it molder in vaults, stash it away in archives, or publish it for all the world to see—even if that's not what the author intended? The problem crops up more often than you might think, since most authors have many less-than-polished drafts hiding somewhere in their files. And while some authors have asked for unfinished work to be destroyed, doing so just might deprive the world of a treasure.

Take Franz Kafka: We would have very little of his works if it weren't for his rebellious friend and fellow writer Max Brod. Kafka didn't publish much during his life, and left his three big novels—*The Trial*, *The Castle*, and *Amerika*—unfinished when he died in 1924. He asked Brod, his literary executor, to destroy them, but Brod disobeyed, to our benefit. Here are other authors who left work unfinished, and the fates of those works.

VLADIMIR NABOKOV //
The Original of Laura

Before he died in 1977, Vladimir Nabokov left behind an unfinished manuscript for a book he tentatively titled *The Original of Laura*. In 138 index cards, the book told the story of an "unnamed 'man of letters' and a nubile twenty-four-year-old," as *The Guardian* put it. In 2008, Nabokov's son Dmitri revealed that his father had given him spectral permission to publish the book. According to Dmitri, his father appeared to him from beyond the grave and said, "You're stuck in a right old mess. Just go ahead and publish."

CHARLES DICKENS //
The Mystery of Edwin Drood

When he died in 1870, Dickens had completed only six of his planned dozen installments for *The Mystery of Edwin Drood*. Unfortunately, his death meant that the identity of the story's murderer was never revealed—but things might have been different, if Queen Victoria had been into spoilers. Three months before his death Dickens sent a letter to the Queen offering to tell her "a little more of it in advance of her subjects." She declined the offer, and now we'll never know what he might have told her. That hasn't stopped at least a dozen people from writing continuations and adaptations, including one from a Vermont printer who claimed to have channeled Dickens's ghost with his "spirit pen."

TRUMAN CAPOTE //
Answered Prayers

During the last years of his life, Truman Capote frequently claimed to be working on a book called *Answered Prayers*. (He signed the contract just two weeks before *In Cold Blood* hit bookstores and became a spectacular success.) But despite repeatedly extended deadlines with his editors and a generous advance, *Answered Prayers* was never completed. In 1971, during an appearance on *The Dick Cavett Show*, Capote referred to it as his "posthumous novel," saying "either I'm going to kill it, or it's going to kill me."

A few chapters of the book were finally published in *Esquire* in 1975 and 1976, with disastrous results: The book was a thinly veiled account of the lifestyles of the rich and famous, many of whom were Capote's friends. Stunned after recognizing themselves in the chapters, most of Capote's friends abandoned him—sending the writer into a depressive spiral of drugs and alcohol from which some say he never recovered.

The book's remaining chapters are something of a mystery. They may still be languishing in a safe deposit box somewhere (some think they're in a locker at the Los Angeles Greyhound Bus Depot). Others think they may have never existed, despite all of Capote's talk. Nevertheless, three of the chapters from *Esquire* were published in book form in 1987 (three years after Capote died) under the title *Answered Prayers: The Unfinished Novel*. Critics weren't kind.

Books I Couldn't Finish

1
TITLE: _____
AUTHOR: _____
WHY: _____
_____

2
TITLE: _____
AUTHOR: _____
WHY: _____
_____

3
TITLE: _____
AUTHOR: _____
WHY: _____
_____

4
TITLE: _____
AUTHOR: _____
WHY: _____
_____

Bart's Books is said to be the largest independently owned and operated outdoor bookstore in the world. Richard Bartinsdale opened the store in Ojai, California, in the '60s, when he found his personal collection was getting overwhelming. Bartinsdale initially used coffee cans instead of a register; the honor system is still in place today. With books as cheap as 35 cents, it's easy enough to cough up the change.

IF I COULD DESIGN A BOOKSTORE,
IT WOULD HAVE

I WOULD CALL IT

A Place I Love to Read

Writing in Fort Greene Park

Richard Wright wrote most of his influential 1940 novel *Native Son* on a yellow legal pad sitting on a bench in Brooklyn's Fort Greene Park. There is now a park bench dedicated to the writer, inscribed with his line about the novel: "In the writing of scene after scene I was guided by but one criterion: to tell the truth as I saw it."

In 2017, the New York City Mayor's Office of Media and Entertainment announced a city-wide book club called "One Book, One New York," which encouraged everyone in New York City to read the same book at the same time. Fifty thousand votes were cast and determined that Chimamanda Ngozi Adichie's *Americanah*—which follows a young woman named Ifemelu as she leaves Nigeria for the United States to attend college—would be the first read. When asked about New York's choice in an interview with HuffPost, Adichie said she was honored, and likened the idea of the whole city reading the same book to "the idea of a village gathering under a tree in the moonlight and telling their stories."

3 BOOKS THAT WOULD BE GREAT FOR BOOK CLUB

TITLE: _____

_____

AUTHOR: _____

· ·

TITLE: _____

_____

AUTHOR: _____

· ·

TITLE: _____

_____

AUTHOR: _____

If you want to truly be surrounded by books, consider visiting **Livraria da Vila**, a São Paulo, Brazil, bookstore that is located in a former home reimagined by architect Isay Weinfeld. Not only does Livraria da Vila have areas where books cover the space from floor to ceiling, there's also a large circular hole between the first floor and basement that's lined in books. Even the entrance is made of bookshelves—which, when closed, make it look as though there are no doors at all.

MAGNA LIBRIS

BOOKSTORES
AROUND THE WORLD
I'D LIKE TO VISIT

NAME: _____

LOCATION: _____

WHY: _____
_____
_____
_____
_____

NAME: _____

LOCATION: _____

WHY: _____
_____
_____
_____
_____
_____

NAME: _____

LOCATION: _____

WHY: _____
_____
_____
_____
_____
_____

NAME: _____

LOCATION: _____

WHY: _____
_____
_____
_____
_____

NAME: _____

LOCATION: _____

WHY: _____
_____
_____
_____
_____

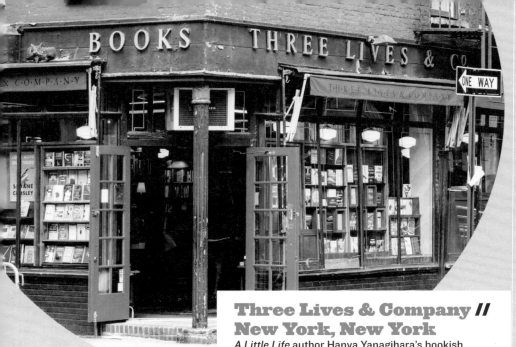

Three Lives & Company // New York, New York

A Little Life author Hanya Yanagihara's bookish heart belongs to New York City's Three Lives & Company. "[It] is the kind of tiny, cheery bookshop that exists only in movies, and that people come to New York hoping to find," Yanagihara says of the West Village shop.

Country Bookshelf // Bozeman, Montana

Growing up near Montana's largest independent bookstore helped shape *Lafayette in the Somewhat United States* author Sarah Vowell's love of words at an early age. She cites Country Bookshelf as one of her favorite bookshops "for bogarting my babysitting money throughout my formative years." But she's got a few other stores vying for the top spot, including: Politics and Prose in Washington, D.C.; The Elliott Bay Book Company in Seattle; Powell's Books in Portland, Oregon; and "an honorable mention to Eslite in Taiwan for making book shopping second only to dumpling eating as Taipei's favorite pastime."

Bookstores I Love

NAME: _____

LOCATION: _____

NAME: _____

LOCATION: _____

NAME: _____

LOCATION: _____

NAME: _____

LOCATION: _____

NAME: _____

LOCATION: _____

NAME: _____

LOCATION: _____

Murder by the Book // Houston, Texas

Bestselling crime author Megan Abbott has favorite bookstores in a range of categories. When it comes to what the author of *The Turnout*, *Give Me Your Hand*, and *The Fever* classifies as her "favorite bookstore-for-whom-my-debt-is-the-greatest, it'd be Murder by the Book in Houston, its extraordinary owner McKenna Jordan, and its brilliant booksellers. They serve as one of the great beacons of light in the crime-fiction community. And they always recommend the best books to me. I never leave empty-handed."

BOOK CLUB LOG

TITLE: _____

DATE: _____

CHOSEN BY: _____

THOUGHTS: _____

_____

_____

_____

RATINGS

CHARACTERS
☆ ☆ ☆ ☆ ☆

PLOT DEVELOPMENT
☆ ☆ ☆ ☆ ☆

QUALITY OF WRITING
☆ ☆ ☆ ☆ ☆

OVERALL
☆ ☆ ☆ ☆ ☆

TITLE: _____

DATE: _____

CHOSEN BY: _____

THOUGHTS: _____

_____

_____

_____

RATINGS

CHARACTERS
☆ ☆ ☆ ☆ ☆

PLOT DEVELOPMENT
☆ ☆ ☆ ☆ ☆

QUALITY OF WRITING
☆ ☆ ☆ ☆ ☆

OVERALL
☆ ☆ ☆ ☆ ☆

TITLE: _____

DATE: _____

CHOSEN BY: _____

THOUGHTS: _____

_____

_____

_____

RATINGS

CHARACTERS
☆ ☆ ☆ ☆ ☆

PLOT DEVELOPMENT
☆ ☆ ☆ ☆ ☆

QUALITY OF WRITING
☆ ☆ ☆ ☆ ☆

OVERALL
☆ ☆ ☆ ☆ ☆

TITLE: _____

DATE: _____

CHOSEN BY: _____

THOUGHTS: _____

_____

_____

_____

RATINGS

CHARACTERS
☆ ☆ ☆ ☆ ☆

PLOT DEVELOPMENT
☆ ☆ ☆ ☆ ☆

QUALITY OF WRITING
☆ ☆ ☆ ☆ ☆

OVERALL
☆ ☆ ☆ ☆ ☆

TITLE: _____

DATE: _____

CHOSEN BY: _____

THOUGHTS: _____

_____

_____

_____

RATINGS

CHARACTERS
☆ ☆ ☆ ☆ ☆

PLOT DEVELOPMENT
☆ ☆ ☆ ☆ ☆

QUALITY OF WRITING
☆ ☆ ☆ ☆ ☆

OVERALL
☆ ☆ ☆ ☆ ☆

TITLE: _____

DATE: _____

CHOSEN BY: _____

THOUGHTS: _____

_____

_____

_____

RATINGS

CHARACTERS
☆ ☆ ☆ ☆ ☆

PLOT DEVELOPMENT
☆ ☆ ☆ ☆ ☆

QUALITY OF WRITING
☆ ☆ ☆ ☆ ☆

OVERALL
☆ ☆ ☆ ☆ ☆

"She is too fond of books, and it has turned her brain."

—LOUISA MAY ALCOTT, *Work: A Story of Experience*

TITLE: _____

DATE: _____

CHOSEN BY: _____

THOUGHTS: _____

_____

_____

_____

RATINGS

CHARACTERS
☆ ☆ ☆ ☆ ☆

PLOT DEVELOPMENT
☆ ☆ ☆ ☆ ☆

QUALITY OF WRITING
☆ ☆ ☆ ☆ ☆

OVERALL
☆ ☆ ☆ ☆ ☆

TITLE: _____

DATE: _____

CHOSEN BY: _____

THOUGHTS: _____

_____

_____

_____

RATINGS

CHARACTERS
☆ ☆ ☆ ☆ ☆

PLOT DEVELOPMENT
☆ ☆ ☆ ☆ ☆

QUALITY OF WRITING
☆ ☆ ☆ ☆ ☆

OVERALL
☆ ☆ ☆ ☆ ☆

"Authors like cats because they are such quiet, lovable, wise creatures, and cats like authors for the same reasons."

—ROBERTSON DAVIES

TITLE: _____

DATE: _____

CHOSEN BY: _____

THOUGHTS: _____

_____

_____

_____

RATINGS

CHARACTERS
☆ ☆ ☆ ☆ ☆

PLOT DEVELOPMENT
☆ ☆ ☆ ☆ ☆

QUALITY OF WRITING
☆ ☆ ☆ ☆ ☆

OVERALL
☆ ☆ ☆ ☆ ☆

TITLE: _____

DATE: _____

CHOSEN BY: _____

THOUGHTS: _____

_____

_____

_____

RATINGS

CHARACTERS
☆ ☆ ☆ ☆ ☆

PLOT DEVELOPMENT
☆ ☆ ☆ ☆ ☆

QUALITY OF WRITING
☆ ☆ ☆ ☆ ☆

OVERALL
☆ ☆ ☆ ☆ ☆

TITLE: _____

DATE: _____

CHOSEN BY: _____

THOUGHTS: _____
_____
_____
_____

RATINGS

CHARACTERS
☆ ☆ ☆ ☆ ☆

PLOT DEVELOPMENT
☆ ☆ ☆ ☆ ☆

QUALITY OF WRITING
☆ ☆ ☆ ☆ ☆

OVERALL
☆ ☆ ☆ ☆ ☆

TITLE: _____

DATE: _____

CHOSEN BY: _____

THOUGHTS: _____
_____
_____
_____

RATINGS

CHARACTERS
☆ ☆ ☆ ☆ ☆

PLOT DEVELOPMENT
☆ ☆ ☆ ☆ ☆

QUALITY OF WRITING
☆ ☆ ☆ ☆ ☆

OVERALL
☆ ☆ ☆ ☆ ☆

TITLE: _____

DATE: _____

CHOSEN BY: _____

THOUGHTS: _____
_____
_____
_____

RATINGS

CHARACTERS
☆ ☆ ☆ ☆ ☆

PLOT DEVELOPMENT
☆ ☆ ☆ ☆ ☆

QUALITY OF WRITING
☆ ☆ ☆ ☆ ☆

OVERALL
☆ ☆ ☆ ☆ ☆

> ## "All great artists draw from the same resource: the human heart, which tells us all that we are more alike than we are unalike."
>
> —MAYA ANGELOU, _Letter to My Daughter_

BOOK CLUB LOG

TITLE: _____

DATE: _____

CHOSEN BY: _____

THOUGHTS: _____

_____

_____

_____

RATINGS

CHARACTERS

☆ ☆ ☆ ☆ ☆

PLOT DEVELOPMENT

☆ ☆ ☆ ☆ ☆

QUALITY OF WRITING

☆ ☆ ☆ ☆ ☆

OVERALL

☆ ☆ ☆ ☆ ☆

TITLE: _____

DATE: _____

CHOSEN BY: _____

THOUGHTS: _____

_____

_____

_____

RATINGS

CHARACTERS

☆ ☆ ☆ ☆ ☆

PLOT DEVELOPMENT

☆ ☆ ☆ ☆ ☆

QUALITY OF WRITING

☆ ☆ ☆ ☆ ☆

OVERALL

☆ ☆ ☆ ☆ ☆

TITLE: _____

DATE: _____

CHOSEN BY: _____

THOUGHTS: _____

_____

_____

_____

RATINGS

CHARACTERS

☆ ☆ ☆ ☆ ☆

PLOT DEVELOPMENT

☆ ☆ ☆ ☆ ☆

QUALITY OF WRITING

☆ ☆ ☆ ☆ ☆

OVERALL

☆ ☆ ☆ ☆ ☆

TITLE: _____

DATE: _____

CHOSEN BY: _____

THOUGHTS: _____

_____

_____

_____

RATINGS

CHARACTERS

☆ ☆ ☆ ☆ ☆

PLOT DEVELOPMENT

☆ ☆ ☆ ☆ ☆

QUALITY OF WRITING

☆ ☆ ☆ ☆ ☆

OVERALL

☆ ☆ ☆ ☆ ☆

TITLE: _____

DATE: _____

CHOSEN BY: _____

THOUGHTS: _____

_____

_____

_____

RATINGS

CHARACTERS
☆ ☆ ☆ ☆ ☆

PLOT DEVELOPMENT
☆ ☆ ☆ ☆ ☆

QUALITY OF WRITING
☆ ☆ ☆ ☆ ☆

OVERALL
☆ ☆ ☆ ☆ ☆

> ## "I have always imagined that Paradise will be a kind of library."
> ### —JORGE LUIS BORGES

TITLE: _____

DATE: _____

CHOSEN BY: _____

THOUGHTS: _____

_____

_____

_____

RATINGS

CHARACTERS
☆ ☆ ☆ ☆ ☆

PLOT DEVELOPMENT
☆ ☆ ☆ ☆ ☆

QUALITY OF WRITING
☆ ☆ ☆ ☆ ☆

OVERALL
☆ ☆ ☆ ☆ ☆

TITLE: _____

DATE: _____

CHOSEN BY: _____

THOUGHTS: _____

_____

_____

_____

RATINGS

CHARACTERS
☆ ☆ ☆ ☆ ☆

PLOT DEVELOPMENT
☆ ☆ ☆ ☆ ☆

QUALITY OF WRITING
☆ ☆ ☆ ☆ ☆

OVERALL
☆ ☆ ☆ ☆ ☆

TITLE: _____
DATE: _____
CHOSEN BY: _____
THOUGHTS: _____
_____
_____
_____

RATINGS

CHARACTERS
☆ ☆ ☆ ☆ ☆

PLOT DEVELOPMENT
☆ ☆ ☆ ☆ ☆

QUALITY OF WRITING
☆ ☆ ☆ ☆ ☆

OVERALL
☆ ☆ ☆ ☆ ☆

TITLE: _____
DATE: _____
CHOSEN BY: _____
THOUGHTS: _____
_____
_____
_____

RATINGS

CHARACTERS
☆ ☆ ☆ ☆ ☆

PLOT DEVELOPMENT
☆ ☆ ☆ ☆ ☆

QUALITY OF WRITING
☆ ☆ ☆ ☆ ☆

OVERALL
☆ ☆ ☆ ☆ ☆

TITLE: _____
DATE: _____
CHOSEN BY: _____
THOUGHTS: _____
_____
_____
_____

RATINGS

CHARACTERS
☆ ☆ ☆ ☆ ☆

PLOT DEVELOPMENT
☆ ☆ ☆ ☆ ☆

QUALITY OF WRITING
☆ ☆ ☆ ☆ ☆

OVERALL
☆ ☆ ☆ ☆ ☆

"**There is hardly any grief that an hour's reading will not dissipate.**"

—BARON DE MONTESQUIEU

> **"Books are a form of political action. Books are knowledge. Books are reflection. Books change your mind."**
>
> —TONI MORRISON, interview, *Word Magazine*

TITLE: _____

DATE: _____

CHOSEN BY: _____

THOUGHTS: _____

_____

_____

_____

RATINGS

CHARACTERS
☆ ☆ ☆ ☆ ☆

PLOT DEVELOPMENT
☆ ☆ ☆ ☆ ☆

QUALITY OF WRITING
☆ ☆ ☆ ☆ ☆

OVERALL
☆ ☆ ☆ ☆ ☆

TITLE: _____

DATE: _____

CHOSEN BY: _____

THOUGHTS: _____

_____

_____

_____

RATINGS

CHARACTERS
☆ ☆ ☆ ☆ ☆

PLOT DEVELOPMENT
☆ ☆ ☆ ☆ ☆

QUALITY OF WRITING
☆ ☆ ☆ ☆ ☆

OVERALL
☆ ☆ ☆ ☆ ☆

TITLE: _____

DATE: _____

CHOSEN BY: _____

THOUGHTS: _____

_____

_____

_____

RATINGS

CHARACTERS
☆ ☆ ☆ ☆ ☆

PLOT DEVELOPMENT
☆ ☆ ☆ ☆ ☆

QUALITY OF WRITING
☆ ☆ ☆ ☆ ☆

OVERALL
☆ ☆ ☆ ☆ ☆

TITLE: _____

DATE: _____

CHOSEN BY: _____

THOUGHTS: _____
_____
_____
_____

RATINGS

CHARACTERS
☆ ☆ ☆ ☆ ☆

PLOT DEVELOPMENT
☆ ☆ ☆ ☆ ☆

QUALITY OF WRITING
☆ ☆ ☆ ☆ ☆

OVERALL
☆ ☆ ☆ ☆ ☆

TITLE: _____

DATE: _____

CHOSEN BY: _____

THOUGHTS: _____
_____
_____
_____

RATINGS

CHARACTERS
☆ ☆ ☆ ☆ ☆

PLOT DEVELOPMENT
☆ ☆ ☆ ☆ ☆

QUALITY OF WRITING
☆ ☆ ☆ ☆ ☆

OVERALL
☆ ☆ ☆ ☆ ☆

TITLE: _____

DATE: _____

CHOSEN BY: _____

THOUGHTS: _____
_____
_____
_____

RATINGS

CHARACTERS
☆ ☆ ☆ ☆ ☆

PLOT DEVELOPMENT
☆ ☆ ☆ ☆ ☆

QUALITY OF WRITING
☆ ☆ ☆ ☆ ☆

OVERALL
☆ ☆ ☆ ☆ ☆

"If a book is well written I always find it too short."

—JANE AUSTEN, "Catharine, or the Bower"

> **"What really knocks me out is a book that, when you're all done reading it, you wish the author that wrote it was a terrific friend of yours and you could call him up on the phone whenever you felt like it."**
>
> —J.D. SALINGER, *The Catcher in the Rye*

TITLE: _____

DATE: _____

CHOSEN BY: _____

THOUGHTS: _____

_____

_____

_____

RATINGS

CHARACTERS
☆ ☆ ☆ ☆ ☆

PLOT DEVELOPMENT
☆ ☆ ☆ ☆ ☆

QUALITY OF WRITING
☆ ☆ ☆ ☆ ☆

OVERALL
☆ ☆ ☆ ☆ ☆

TITLE: _____

DATE: _____

CHOSEN BY: _____

THOUGHTS: _____

_____

_____

_____

RATINGS

CHARACTERS
☆ ☆ ☆ ☆ ☆

PLOT DEVELOPMENT
☆ ☆ ☆ ☆ ☆

QUALITY OF WRITING
☆ ☆ ☆ ☆ ☆

OVERALL
☆ ☆ ☆ ☆ ☆

TITLE: _____

DATE: _____

CHOSEN BY: _____

THOUGHTS: _____

_____

_____

_____

RATINGS

CHARACTERS
☆ ☆ ☆ ☆ ☆

PLOT DEVELOPMENT
☆ ☆ ☆ ☆ ☆

QUALITY OF WRITING
☆ ☆ ☆ ☆ ☆

OVERALL
☆ ☆ ☆ ☆ ☆